KINCAIDIANA
A Flute Player's Notebook

William Morris Kincaid, 1895-1967
(Photo by Adrian Siegel)

KINCAIDIANA
A Flute Player's Notebook

SECOND EDITION

JOHN C. KRELL

with a foreword by
William R. Smith
Former Assistant Conductor, The Philadelphia Orchestra

The National Flute Association, Inc.
Santa Clarita, California

© Copyright 1973, 1997 by John C. Krell
All rights reserved. No part of this publication
may be reproduced, stored in a retrieval system, or
transmitted in any form or by any means, elecronic, mechanical,
photocopying, recording, or otherwise, without the prior permission of
The National Flute Association, Inc.

BOOK DESIGN: ROBERT E. SHEPARD
DESIGN, SECOND EDITION: SUZANNE THIERRY
EDITOR, SECOND EDITION: NANCY TOFF

Published by
The National Flute Association, Inc.
P.O. Box 800592
Santa Clarita, CA 91380-0597

ISBN 0-9657904-0-1
Printed in U.S.A.

CONTENTS

Preface to the Second Edition vii
Preface ix
Foreword by William R. Smith xiii

PART I—Elements of Technique 1
Diaphragm and Resonance 2
Embouchure 5
Tone 7
Relative Intensity 13
Vibrato 14
Articulation 17
Finger Technique 22

PART II—Phrasing 29
Song vs. Dance Elements 30
Phrase Groupings 31
Legato Intervals 38
Line 42

PART III—Some Elements of Musical Execution 49
Rhythm 50
Tempos 53
Breathing Points 55
Dynamics 57
Fake Fingering 58
Ornaments 59
Couplets 60
Memorization 61
Ensemble 61

PART IV—A Final Word 63
The Flute Repertoire 64
Postlude 65

Appendixes 69
A. Factors in Tone Production 71
B. Daily Practice Routines and Materials.. 75
C. The Flutist's Repertoire 81
D. Difference Tones 87
E. The Piccolo: An Artist's Approach 92
F. "William M. Kincaid"
   from *The Flutist,* June 1925 101
G. Interview with William Kincaid,
   May 1960—*Hope E. Stoddard* 102
H. Reminiscences of William Kincaid—
   Kenton Terry 110
I. Reminiscences of William Kincaid—
   Sol Schoenbach 116
J. Discography of Solo
   and Chamber Recordings by
   William Kincaid—*John Solum* 119
Index 125

PREFACE TO THE SECOND EDITION

It is difficult to realize that more than a half century has passed since the notes for this book were first scribbled out and subsequently organized into typewritten pages under my title of *Kincaidiana*. There were no thoughts of publication, and at that time there was little information about the flute being circulated—no master classes, no *Flutist Quarterlies*, no flute conventions, few flute recitals, and, for that matter, few good teachers around. Consequently, these anonymous notes were shared with friends, who in turn shared them with their friends until a sort of national circulation evolved. To my great regret, however, the notes were sometimes mistakenly ascribed verbatim to Kincaid himself, which was a great injustice to him and certainly a great embarrassment to me. He was a very private and particular man, and, although very articulate, he was most hesitant to put anything down in writing. We members of the Philadelphia Orchestra flute section used to try to persuade him to edit some flute music, but he always demurred, saying, "What if I wake up some morning and want to change it?" He was flexible in his phrasing and refused to lock himself in to just one interpretation. He was seldom clinical in his teaching and was always more concerned with the musicality than the methodology.

When the book was finally published in 1973, I fully expected it would live a short life due to the timeliness of the subject and its restricted audience.

Much to my astonishment, the book has not only endured in the flute world but has had some general application in other instrumental and vocal fields, including a surprising appeal to percussionists.

If nothing more comes of it, I hope that this book will persuade the reader that music is a visceral, expressive medium which requires a personal involvement on the part of the performer. Far from being a perfection of technique and a literal reading of the notation, music is full of little propulsions, progressions, impulses, inflections, and other musical gestures, too subtle to indicate in the notation, but without which the performance would be static and lifeless. These minuscule liberties are generally taken within the pulse so that the metric frame of the bar remains, and the small freedoms taken are almost obscured. Kincaid used to say, "Think it, but don't quite do it." Casals described performance as playing ever so slightly "out of time." And Tabuteau always admonished us to play "between the notes." Please understand that I am not talking about rubatos, ritards, accelerandos, etc., but rather about a subtle, elastic flexibility that serves to reinforce the rhythm and movement of the music.

Of course, performance customs change over time (vibratos, tempos, styles, and even the instruments themselves), but there are certain basic musical values that endure through it all—and that is what this little book is all about.

John C. Krell
October 1996

PREFACE

For almost forty years the distinct style and sound, the lively musical intelligence, the shock of platinum hair, the ruddy complexion and the courtly manner of the renowned flutist, Mr. William Morris Kincaid, was a fixture and trademark of the Philadelphia Orchestra. To a great degree, he was responsible for developing a robust style that might be called the American school of flute playing. Mr. James A. Maggillivray defines it as follows:

> "A distinctively American style of playing is now just beginning to appear with the rise of the first generation of American-born principals in the important orchestras. Their teachers, like Tabuteau and Gillet on the oboe, Barrère on the flute, were mostly of the less exuberantly French kind, and the present movement is towards continued restraint, with stress on blending rather than contrasting colours, but with the French roots clearly showing, even though many eminent clarinettists are of Italian origin. The magnificent Kincaid of the Philadelphia Orchestra combines French flute virtues with a more virile quality which is all his own, and which against all precedent sounds equally appropriate in Beethoven and in César Franck."[1]

[1] Anthony Baines, ed., *Musical Instruments Through The Ages* (Baltimore: Penguin Books, 1961), pg. 268.

More than a superlative flutist, Mr. Kincaid was the complete musician and a great teacher. His contagious enthusiasm for the instrument fired a couple generations of American flutists and his pupils, and pupils of his pupils, are now solo flutists or fill sections of orchestras all over the world.[1] His many, many students knew him as an extremely articulate man, which makes it all the more a pity that he never put down in writing what he so aptly expressed in lessons.

As one of his teaching techniques, he used to insist that his students keep notes, always threatening to examine them but seldom getting around to it. My notes were kept haphazardly during the period 1939-41 while a flute student at the Curtis Institute of Music in Philadelphia; they accumulated on old scraps of paper and on the backs of used envelopes until I was embarrassed enough by the clutter to assemble them during an inactive period of Army Service in 1945. These anonymous notes, under my title of "Kincaidiana," were loaned to friends and then copied and distributed by friends till they became a kind of underground publication without credit, or, more important, responsibility. Recently, Mr. Richard A. Condon, after determining that I was the source of the notes, suggested that the material be published.

This involved a reexamination of the notes, which in turn suggested a complete reworking to eliminate some of the more extravagant generalizations that go with the brashness of youth and to amplify other short-hand observations incompletely described in the original. However, it must be understood that these notes are not a quoting of

---

[1] A partial list is given in an interview with Kincaid on pg. 102.

chapter and verse on Mr. Kincaid, but rather an attempt to explain back to myself the musical values and philosophies he inspired. As such there are subjective interpretations involved, although all of the root ideas stem directly from Kincaid's musical intelligence and artistry.

During the Curtis period I participated in the now legendary ensemble classes of the eminent oboist Marcel Tabuteau. In retrospect, I can see that many of his concepts filtered into the notes. This is appropriate since the musical ideas of these two men overlapped and supplemented each other to a remarkable degree. Mr. Kincaid would speak of "relative intensity" while Mr. Tabuteau spoke of "speed of wind." Kincaid worked with "phrase groupings" whereas Tabuteau described the same groupings in terms of "number sequences" and "impulses." By musical osmosis I am sure that other observations have unconsciously crept into these notes due to the influences of colleagues, conductors and guest artists over many years of making music together.

Although my notes were not originally intended for publication, I have reproduced them here because of a feeling of responsibility to conserve a part of the Kincaid legacy for future generations of flutists. The ideal *Kincaidiana* would be a compendium of all his students' notes. Many others, by reason of exposure and periods of study, might be better qualified; however, by default, I happen to be the one.

In the first section of the book I discuss the elements of flute technique; in the second, I show how Mr. Kincaid applied these tools of the trade to his more philosophical ideas of phrasing and line; and in the third I have covered a series of points of musical execution. It is my hope that they will be provocative, and even controversial, encouraging thought and analysis about tone, phrasing and performance.

I acknowledge with thanks the helpful suggestions and comments of my friends and colleagues John de Lancie, Sol Schoenbach, William R. Smith and Kenton F. Terry. Thanks also to Eileen Anderson for her able assistance in preparing the manuscript and to my aunt, Augusta E. Howell, for her help in eliminating some of my superfluous punctuation. Permission of Adrian Siegel and Thomas and Walter L. Wolf to reproduce the photographs is much appreciated.

I am particularly indebted to Richard A. Condon for searching out the original notes and for his encouragement in revising them for publication.

In this latest resuscitation of the book, I would like to acknowledge the help and encouragement of Nancy Toff, Kathy Borst Jones, and John Solum in all the complications involved in its reprinting process.

John C. Krell

Foreword

A stone thrown upon the surface of still waters; the beauty of ever-enlarging circles of influence evolving endlessly.

A familiar image, and still the most apt for the impact of a great man upon his time.

But, as the circles grow larger they also grow weaker; it is necessary for someone to concentrate attention upon the achievements before they grow imperceptible.

William Kincaid was a great flutist, and he was a great teacher. He trained many great flutists, but far fewer great teachers. One man who happily combines both talents is John Krell, who has done so much to keep the light a-flame, the wonder that was Kincaid alive.

How fortunate we are to have these notes and explanations, these marvels and revelations, thanks to Krell's burr-like memory, as well as an orderly mind which kept notes through years of study, and refined the ideas in years of teaching.

Kincaid's theories "worked," as all flutists well know, and the elaboration of them in this invaluable volume assures us that the widening circles of his influence will continue to spread throughout the world of music.

William R. Smith
Assistant Conductor,
The Philadelphia Orchestra

Kincaid at a recording session of the Philadelphia Orchestra.

Part I
Elements of Technique

DIAPHRAGM AND RESONANCE

One of the happy aspects of music is the complete individuality, difference and variety in the qualities of performers' tones. It is possible to play or sing *like* someone else, but quite impossible to duplicate perfectly another's tone because of the great variety of differences in physical equipment. This is particularly true of wind players where such variables as the size of the lips, the shape of the mouth, the resonances of the throat and the configuration of the rib cage, to name a few, precondition the timbre of tone produced. It is up to each player to exploit what he has in the way of biological and anatomical endowment to its fullest advantage. The analogy to voice is obvious, and the flutist should take advantage of all vocal concepts and techniques.[1]

Tone production begins with the diaphragm. The diaphragm is the flutist's "bow." The thorough development of this muscle and the musculature surrounding it is basic. Just as a good violinist plays *in* the string and not just on the surface, it follows that a flutist must develop a supported sound with substance and depth and not just a superficial thread of sound. The tone of the flute is supported by the diaphragm. If there is a secret to playing, it is simply letting the diaphragm-supported flow of air produce the sounds while the lips merely shape or grip the air without crushing it. The process requires a real physical involvement and effort of all the muscles of breathing. It takes more than a shallow, conversational breath to produce a convincing, live

---

[1] I frequently refer my more curious students to William Venard's syllabus *Singing: the Mechanism and the Technic* (New York: Carl Fischer, 1969). There are two excellent chapters on breathing and resonance that are particularly pertinent.

tone on the flute. At all times the diaphragm must be firm and controlled so that you can push for intensity, support for continuity of sound, give little kicks for *staccatos* or gentle nudges for expressive accents.

Think of tone in terms of a cork ball supported in the air by a column of compressed air. Tone is like this ball. Once suspended, it need only be supported by the breath. An excellent exercise is to stretch out on your back and place a heavy weight (10 lbs. or so) on the diaphragm just below the floating ribs.[1] Push the weight up quickly as you inhale, make an embouchure and then exhale slowly against the resistance of the lips as the weight descends, maintaining a firm muscle tone all the while so as to distribute the air evenly. Do this 10 times then rest; 10 times, rest; 10 times, rest; 10 times, rest—forty times in all till the procedure becomes reflexive and automatic. (You never really learn anything until you can forget it!) Keep the abdominal muscles relaxed as you inhale to allow the floor of the diaphragm to descend. On exhalation press these same abdominal muscles somewhat against the resistance of the diaphragm so as to control the distribution of the air. Swimming is recommended, too, for it forces you to breathe with the diaphragm. Practice panting at a rapid pace for this reminds you of the diaphragmatic activity involved and prepares you for the control of the small jabs useful in *staccato* articulations.

The military, chest-heaving style of breathing not only restricts control of the air because of the weight of the descending rib cage, but cuts out

---

[1] One of my students had remarkable success with this exercise by placing her baby brother on her diaphragm.

half of the resonance in the process. Keep the chest up but not in an artificially elevated army "brace." Do not allow it to become concave.

Open and create as much space as possible in the mouth, particularly for the middle E and for the low register articulations. Experiment with the effects that various vowel resonances (A, E, I, O, U and Y) can have in modulating the tone quality. *Always* play with a relaxed, open throat. Yawn just before starting a sound to get this feeling of openness. Even the tongue may play a part. For example, to assist in playing ascending diminuendo scale passages, place the tip at the base of the lower teeth and arch the remainder toward the roof of the mouth.

In general, avoid *any* constriction in the column of air as it is pushed up from the floor of the diaphragm through the chest, throat and mouth to the resistance of the mouthpiece of the lips. Imagine your body to be as hollow as possible and think of blowing up from the floor. Search for that flattering resonance which you may have experienced at some time when you hummed or sang in a small, enclosed space (as in a shower stall) and were rewarded with a wonderful fullness of sound in your ears. Search for this ring in your tone by exploring the resonant cavities of your body. Remember that in the final analysis, *you* are the source of the flute's sound; so cultivate the sensation of the tone being generated *by* the diaphragm and sounding *inside* the body.

EMBOUCHURE

Since the flutist has no built-in resistance in the form of a reed or mouthpiece, he must make his own mouthpiece by building this resistance in the musculature of the lips themselves so as to contain, shape and aim the column of air that is pressed against them. Additional resistance can be obtained by directing the air stream somewhat more *at* the opposite wall than over it. Aim the air stream down for the lower and more across for the upper registers.

The embouchure might be described as a simultaneous stretch and pucker (like trying to smile and whistle at the same time), or as the shape the lips assume when blowing to cool a hot drink. The precise placement of the flute in relationship to the lip is crucial. Brush the flute *up* to the lip and do not crush down on the red portion from above as this positioning inhibits the flexibility of the lower lip. Place the embouchure plate comfortably into the natural indentation of the jaw, allowing the lower lip to overlap slightly. Cover as much of the plate to each side as possible, so that the opening of the lips is long, straight and thin rather than round and open. For the low register, stretch the lips somewhat at the corners, covering about a fourth of the mouth hole and directing the air downward. As you ascend to the upper octaves, relax the corners of the lip, compress them gently forward, pucker over and across the hole and direct the air more across the hole. Keep the cheeks relaxed. The only facial muscles that should be exerted are those immediately around the perimeter of the lips. Play from the smooth, moist inside of the lips and work for an open tone—open, that is, in the sense of not being constricted or forced, particularly in the low register.

Each flutist's facial structure, teeth, lips, etc., are so individual that the formation of the embouchure can be specified only in these most general terms.[1]

Make a habit of clearing the lips of any saliva by moistening them by a flick of the tongue whenever you breathe, and always before you start to play. This is especially important when starting difficult pianissimos in the low octave. The lubrication has the additional advantage of smoothing out any little wrinkles or chappings in the lips, thus reducing the friction and extraneous dispersion of the flow of air.

The ideal lip aperture is a symmetrical, elliptical opening, certainly no wider than the flute embouchure hole. Any unfocused air is inefficient, creates breathiness in the sound and wastes valuable air. The aperture somewhat resembles the nozzle on a garden hose that can be adjusted to a spray or a concentrated stream of water.[2] Some flutists are plagued by the classic "cupids-bow" lip formation, but many successful players have overcome this handicap by using a "side-winder" embouchure on one side of the mouth.

As a preparation for delicate attacks, it is often helpful to test for the placement of the note by directing a few discreet puffs of air across the hole that are audible only to the player.

---

[1] Mr. Kincaid was never very explicit or clinical about the conformation of the embouchure; he preferred to describe the character of tone desired, leaving it up to the student to search out the quality in terms of his own physical resources.

[2] Rockstro in his excellent and still valid chapter on sound production stresses the importance of the "lip-tube" in conditioning the character of the air stream. See R. S. Rockstro, *A Treatise on the . . . Flute* (London: Rudau, 1928).

By fingering low C and blowing with relaxed lips and the merest breath of air it is possible to produce a wispy arpeggio (G^2, C^3, E^3, G^3, B^{b3}, C^4, D^4, E^4) of "whistle" or "flageolett" sounds that derive from the overtone series. These are not the normal, overblown harmonics but delicate, whispery peanut-whistle sounds that have a remarkably penetrating and eerie quality.[1] This little lip calisthenic makes an excellent warm-up exercise for embouchure placement and breath control (although the whistles should be eliminated when they sound as noises in the tone proper). It is an excellent discipline to try to isolate one note from the whistle series and sustain it for ten seconds. The slightest change in breath support will flick you to one of the adjoining whistle notes. Flageolett harmonics are obtainable over other low register notes and can also be produced with the regular third octave fingerings, with which you can improvise little whistle tunes.

TONE

We all strive for a "good tone," but in practice a good tone is that particular quality which is appropriate to the period, style or character of the music being performed—e.g., the raw energy of a Beethoven, the diaphanous pastels of a Debussy or the harvest colors of a Brahms. Since much of music is sheer sensory imagery and intimately involved with our world of physical and psychical experience, ideally tone should be able to reflect life impressions such as motion, tension, relaxation, excitement, repose, anguish, joy, beauty, etc.

---

[1] These flageoletts were actually scored for flute in a concerto written for Mr. Kincaid by Louis Gesensway, a violinist-composer in the Philadelphia Orchestra.

Traditionally, the flute has been identified with pan-pipes and bird calls, salon music with candelabra, and idealized references to gold and silver. As a result, it can become a victim of its own cliché label of "prettiness." But a tone uniformly pretty becomes merely a confection for the ear and loses its emotional value through its sheer consistency. There are moments when the sound should be ravishing and seductive, but others when, if it is to remain faithful to the intent of the music, it should be brittle, intense, *spitzig*, scolding or even unpleasant.[1] It is up to the performer to transcend the trite identifications of his instrument and, instead, communicate the range of meanings which music can have.

Basically, there is a focus to each note of the flute which is its fundamental frequency. Each pitch has its own placement which when achieved brings a maximum response from the instrument. However appropriate it may be at times, this fundamental is a pure tone; as such, it can be bland and characterless. (An orchestra of tuning forks would soon become intolerably dull!) While the flute is relatively deficient in harmonics when compared to the clarinet or oboe, it is still quite possible, particularly in the lower two registers, to manipulate the lips, air pressure and directions of air so as to add (or subtract) a considerable complex of overtones with their interacting resultant, summation and difference tones.[2] Kincaid directed his students to search

---

[1] In past years, the conservatory students used to gather in Verne Q. Powell's studio-office when Mr. Kincaid and the Philadelphia Orchestra were in Boston. They were all eager to impress him with their proficiency but were disconcerted when he asked them to play a cadenza on one note.

[2] For a further understanding of the intricate complexity of sound, read the sensitive paperback by the physicist-flutist, Arthur H. Benade, *Horns, Strings & Harmony* (New York: Doubleday and Co., 1960).

for a "centered" tone—a quality that lies between the extremes of the sharp quality of an open embouchure hole and the flat, smothered quality of a closed hole. He worked for a dark but lively quality that would take the pressure of a supported sound and at the same time avoid the sometimes piercing and strident character of an overly bright sound. It is essential to search for this heart of the tone.

A violinist has at his command the fretting and vibrato of the left hand plus all the resources of the bow—speed and direction, pressure of the wrist, varying contacts with the string and a whole repertoire of intensities depending upon the position of bow in relationship to the finger-board and the bridge. Flutists should emulate these tonal options and try to approximate them. For example, the flute can produce a finger-board *flautando* (lots of loose air across the mouth hole) or a bristly bridge tone (pressure of tight air directed more into the flute) together with all the intermediate intensities.

The recital flutist has much latitude in the dimension of sound, for his range of dynamics is conditioned only by the size and acoustics of the hall and the sensitivity of his accompanist. But modern orchestral playing with its arena halls demands a wide range of dynamics and intensities. It requires a penetrating flute sound of compactness and depth which can be heard above fifty or sixty strings, not to mention the other woodwinds and brass.

The idea of penetration leads us to an important distinction between *volume* and *intensity*. Volume is simply the quantity of air, while intensity is the supported pressure of focused air. A good crescendo-diminuendo line is probably a combination of both, but it is possible to make a note travel by increasing and decreasing intensity (the harmonic content) without appreciably changing the volume, as indicated in the following diagram:

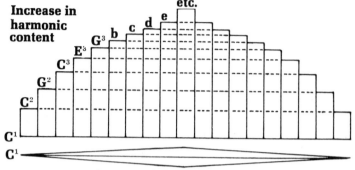

Apparent increase in volume

Intensity makes for penetration and projection. A tone with intensity may sound small at close range, but actually will penetrate much farther than a non-intense tone sounding louder near the ear of the player. This is particularly true of *pianissimos* in which, for projection, the same speed of wind must be maintained as in a *forte* and, in a sense, becomes a slice of the *forte*. Like an actor's stage whispers, *pianissimos* must sound soft but still be heard in the second balcony!

Perhaps the concept of intensity can best be understood in terms of an analogy. Water behaves much like air. Suppose your right hand controls a faucet valve and the left hand controls the nozzle of a garden hose that is directed at the opposite wall of the embouchure hole. If you open the faucet to the maximum pressure and adjust the nozzle so as to get a concentrated stream, you will get a tightly focused column of water impinging against the wall. This is intensity. If, on the other hand, you turn down the pressure and adjust the nozzle to a less concentrated stream, you get a more dispersed pattern against the wall. This is the non-intense, *floatando* sound.

Do not deceive yourself about the intensity of your tone by practicing in a small, vibrant room. If necessary, hang drapes or rugs on the walls to reduce the reverberation. Flutists are so close to the sound that they can never truly hear themselves any more than they can truly hear the sound of their own voices. We must think like actors or public speakers and project the sound outward. Have someone close your ears as you play so that you can listen for the center of the sound. Or pretend you are left-handed and switch the flute around to the opposite side. You will be astonished to hear how differently it sounds to your left ear. Another good idea is to practice facing a corner of a room so that the sound is equally deflected into each ear.

A flutist should develop not only one but many embouchures. Practice blowing out of the sides of the lips for it will give you a greater variety of tone and at the same time strengthen the lip. Tone should not be too direct or too honest. Experiment by blowing obliquely across the mouth hole by pushing the flute forward with the right hand. Sometimes, and particularly in sustained *pianissimos*, you want only vague suggestions of tone, like the diffused focus in photography. To get this veiled *pianissimo*, use lots of air with little grip from the lips, allowing some air in the tone. A violinist gets a similar effect by using yards of bow with little pressure on the string. In some sustained *pianissimo* situations, do not hesitate to use harmonic fingerings. Delicately overblow the octave or the twelfth below (half-holing the note below, in this case, for clearance).[1] The harmonics are not only easier to sustain but often are more appropriate and musical.

[1]For instance, use ● ● ● ○ ● ● ● , for A^2

Intonation, especially in the upper octaves where the frequencies mount, is a lifetime preoccupation of the flutist. Keep a tuning fork handy and hang a bar bell (A-440) in your studio in order to check your A for sympathetic vibration as you practice. Tune without vibrato,[1] adjust to others and eliminate beats.

The second C♯ on the flute is a kind of sharp "wolf" tone, difficult to center and control.[2] Yet, if this note is adjusted for pitch and quality, it will give you an excellent angular placement for the entire flute range. Overblow the lowest C♯ into its octave, then, by rotating the flute, tune and adjust to this pitch with the regular fingering. Lock in the resulting tilt-angle for the entire register.

An easy blowing flute can be tonally disadvantageous, for the instrument will be unable to take the pressure of a good *fortissimo* without allowing the tone to spread. For this reason, the B natural foot joint is a decided advantage, not so much for the very occasional B naturals played, but rather for the added resistance and resonance obtained by the increased length of tube.

The ideal instrument should have a homogeneity of tone throughout its range—that is, there should be no dividing of the scale into registers as such. Instead, the tone quality should be graduated through the natural register breaks so that at no point does a marked change of timbre occur. Some notes (middle C♯, high E and G♯) sound brighter

---

[1] Reputedly, Sir Thomas Beecham, after listening to his oboist's tune A throbbing with a wide vibrato, turned to his orchestra and said, "Gentlemen, take your choice."

[2] If, when you are playing a passage, this C♯ occurs in sufficiently sustained form, you may want to lower its pitch and darken its quality by using one or more fingers of the right hand—e.g.
○ ○ ○ ○ ● ● ●

than their neighbors, but you can darken their quality with the lips or by covering additional holes.

Flute tone, then, is an extremely complex phenomenon capable of great variations and modulations. The flutist should be able to change the color of his tone to suggest perfumes, to indicate textures of light and darkness, to reflect emotions of rage, repose, etc. Tone is one of the most central means of musical communication. Since music has many different kinds of things to say, the flutist should be capable of producing a variety of tonal qualities.

RELATIVE INTENSITY

In addition to its role in modulating the quality of a single note, intensity also helps to identify the relative position of notes in the scale. Just as an aircraft must have a critical flying speed for each altitude, so must each note in the scale have a speed of wind corresponding to its altitude in the range of the flute scale. For instance, a high A to be convincing must sound like a high note and reflect the exertion required for its production. Similarly, a low A must sound low and reflect the velvet repose and relaxation implied by its lowness. Normally, there should be a tension in an ascending scale and a similar relaxation in descending—more pressure of focused air as you rise and more quantity of air as you fall.

In his book *Form and Performance*,[1] Mr. Irwin Stein describes the circumstance thus: "Music ranges over a ladder of eight to nine octaves, but

[1] Stein, Irwin, *Form and Performance*, (Alfred A. Knopf: New York, 1962), pg. 24.

the distinction between low and high notes is relative to the compass of the passage and of the instrument on which it is being performed. The open G string of the violin is a very high note of the double bass; and the high register of a tenor voice, which according to popular appreciation yields some of music's brightest and most brilliant sounds, is within the more or less indifferent middle register of a soprano voice. Whether a note is felt to be high or low does not only depend upon its pitch, but also upon its colour. The act of producing the highest or lowest note, in the voice as well as on many instruments, contributes to its character of brightness or darkness."

Actually, there is more than "brightness" or "darkness" involved. Stravinsky knew precisely what he was doing when he wrote the opening of the *Sacre de Printemps* at the top, strangling range of the bassoon to set the stage for the eerie, primeval atmosphere of the movement. More than that, there is an additional element of empathetic participation on the part of the audience. The listener subconsciously identifies with the performer, strangling along with the bassoon or sharing with the tenor the physical joy of producing a high C in a Puccini climax. If music is a language, this is certainly one of its most important aspects of communication.

VIBRATO

Vibrato is a wonderfully expressive tool when used with taste and discretion. Superficial to the tone itself, the frosting on the cake, it nevertheless adds a lyrical quality and an element of freedom to the flow of sound. Applied intelligently and incorporated into the body of sound, it becomes a very distinctive and individual part of the player's expressive resources.

In practice, however, the vibrato is more noted for its abuse. All too frequently the mechanical, vibraphone type of quaver is superimposed indiscriminately (and continuously) to the extent that the tone becomes all frosting and no cake. Everyone, I am sure, has heard a bass-baritone whose exaggerated quaking destroys all sense of pitch, or the singular church soprano who presides over the whole choir with her own tremulous quality.

To complicate the situation, there is also a kind of mystique about vibrato, some claiming that, with the production of a good, supported sound, it occurs like spontaneous combustion, or that an angel kisses you on the forehead and suddenly there is vibrato! It probably *is* intuitive (we are surrounded by examples), and most likely evolves naturally through imitation of a teacher or a favorite performer. Yet, since it is so personal, many instructors get very evasive and mysterious about its production, hesitating to commit themselves to a specific method of production. The consensus, however, is that it should be a shallow, controlled and even undulation of sound, avoiding the nervous, automatic and uneven type of shaking. It is most probably produced by a combination of the delicate vibration of the throat and the elastic reinforcement of the diaphragm, acting together and sympathetically.

The conscientious musician, like a good string player, will analyze, practice and develop a repertoire of vibrato speeds, contours, amplitudes, intensities and pitch variations, each style subject to the implications of the music being performed. Work with a metronome and start with four pulses of the vibrato a second ($\quarternote = 60$), increasing the speed till a natural rate is found. The average rate is probably around five per second. At times a wide, appassionato vibrato is appropriate (e.g., the solo in the last movement of the Brahms' 1st), but in other circumstances the merest shimmer or insinuation of vibrato is sufficient.

A note can be made to travel by letting the vibrato evolve in speed, amplitude and timbre as the intensity increases (like a flower blossoming). Conversely, one can shift down and dissolve into a straight sound in a diminuendo cadence.

Vibrato also has a bearing on relative intensity considerations (see page 13). The rate of the vibrato pulsation can indicate, to a great degree, the position of the note in the scale. A slower vibrato suggests the relaxation of the low register while a faster rate reinforces the excitement of the top. In other words, the speed of vibrato should be graduated, as we graduate the intensity, through the range of the instrument.

In general, use the vibrato with circumspection. Vibrate on the longer notes and avoid it in running passages; it adds a liquid quality but destroys the line and continuity in the process. Occasionally, a fast quiver of vibrato on a dotted eighth note in a rapid tempo will add to the vitality of the rhythm. A touch of quick vibrato can be used to gently underline the skeletal notes in embellished figurations, or a caressing pulsation can make an accent subtly expressive. In other words, its uses are varied and infinite.

Ideally there should be consensus of vibrato style in each section of an orchestra or ensemble; it takes only one instrument with a machine-gun or heart throb vibrato to destroy the blend of an entire section and disconcert the tuning.

ARTICULATION

Articulation is the pronunciation of musical sound. Although essential, it is a frequently neglected element of musical communication. Articulation makes the music speak and borrows many of its impulses and inflections from life and language. Without this ennunciation music would become monotonous and meaningless, a sustained spaghetti-like sound without shape or form. Each of the instrumental families of the orchestra (strings, winds and percussion) has its own particular techniques of articulation. It is the refinement and sophistication of these specialized startings, durations and releases of sound within the respective instrumental limitations that provide for identification and artistry in performance.[1]

Flutists can learn a great deal about articulation from the strings, who appear to have the greatest variety and option of articulations. With the tremendous bowing potentials of the arm, wrist and fingers, the violinist has an infinitely sophisticated assortment of attacks, sustainings and releases ranging through the *detachés, portés, lourés, lancés, martelés, staccatos,* flying *staccatos, spicattos, ricochets,* etc. — not to mention the subtle but significant difference between the impulses of the up

---

[1]Surprisingly, it is more often the transient noise of articulation than the quality of tone that distinguishes and identifies the instrument.

and down bows. It is instructive and provocative for the flutist to explore bowing techniques in order to approximate the subtleties of violin articulation.[1] All too frequently, the woodwind designations of tonguing are limited to the simple long, medium and short.

If the tone of the violin is introduced by strokes of the bow, the tone of the flute is similarly initiated by the pulses of the diaphragm. These pulses (released by the tongue) can vary from a sigh with gentle, vowel-like beginnings, to a sustained pulse for touch tonguings or quiet "change of bow" tonguings; from soft nudges for the *lourés*, to intermediate punches for the *detachés;* from percussive jabs for the *staccatos* and *marcatos*, to a sustained and supported pulse for the spicatto-like skipping tongue technique of the fast single, mixed, double and triple tonguings. The diaphragm is the flutist's bow and, like the bow, must always be kept in motion. Each articulation, however short, must have a duration and musical value. The diaphragm, in combination with the tongue and the air stream shaped by the lips, is capable of an infinite variety of meaningful impulses, much of it done with the same imagination that is intuitively used in the inflections of speech.

Throughout all this, the tongue plays an essential part, but it must be remembered that it is simply a kind of spring valve that contains and releases the appropriate impulse of pressure of air behind it—sometimes barely audible, sometimes just touching the moving air, sometimes blocking out *detachés* and at others releasing little, miniature *staccato* explosions.

---

[1]Read Chapter III of Ivan Galamian's *Principles of Violin* (Prentice-Hall, Inc.: New York, 1952).

The tongue releases this air from a position on the gum ridge just above the teeth. The syllables used are somewhat limited, mostly those consonant combinations starting with the sharper "T's" (too, tah, toe, etc.) and graduated through to the more gliding and blunt character of the "D's" (doo, dah, doe, etc.). In all instances, the duration is controlled by the pulse of the diaphragm. The ends of the articulation *must* always be kept open. The tone must *never* (except as a special effect) be stopped by the tongue or the lips. In the more sensitive releases, the lip aids in feathering off the tone much as the arm lifts the bow from the string, but in the shorter, *secco staccatos,* the abrupt stop of the diaphragm (again like the bow arm) is indicated.

Since tonguing pressures tend to open the lips, keep them firmer than usual in articulated passages; this will help avoid the sputtering *spitcattos*. Set the embouchure and never nibble the articulations with the jaw or lips; it changes the quality, upsets the placement of tone and, more importantly, slows down the speed. Tongue like a ventriloquist without moving the lips. In the final analysis, articulation is basically the punctuation of a line of sound.

The rhythmical subdivisions of music, far from being a series of static and vertical tick-tocks, are rather horizontal progressions, reflecting the flow and ebb of the musical line. The articulations of the flutist should indicate and shape these accumulations and diminutions of tension and energy by graduating the weight, length and character of these articulations and by resolving the tonguing syllables on the strong rhythmic impulses of the measure, much as we resolve the syllables in speech, e.g., the combination of "to-*doo*" must have the same inflection that we use in pronouncing "to-day." Even when a pick-up "to" is separated from the "doo," it must imply the up impulse and consequent resolution on the "doo." So do not stub your toe or hiccough on these pickups. Mentally superimpose the up and down bowing inflections that preoccupy the string player.

This syllabification is particularly applicable in the rapid, mixed articulation patterns involving dotted rhythms:

When the tempo becomes very rapid, shift to the skipping "ta*re*" or "ta*ruh*" in which case the miniature roll or slap of the tongue resolves the pattern.

Double and triple tonguings are immensely troublesome to some players for pressure and tension accumulate and paralysis sets in as the tempo increases. Here again the solution is the continuity of air and a relaxed tongue just springing away from the pressure of the moving air.[1] It is sometimes a helpful practice to first slur such passages and then superimpose the double tongue on the established breath line. The sharper syllables (te-ke, etc.) tend to chip at the air and musclebind the tongue, hence the blunter sounds of "*doogoo*" for the double and "*doogoodoo*" for the triple tonguings. These blunter syllables help to equalize the discrepancy in attacks and relax the tongue. Practice them in slow motion, for even here the double should be indistinguishable from the single tonguing. For the

---

[1]Double tonguing is analogous to the violinist's *spicatto*, with the bow always in motion.

more staccato and rapid passages, a bit sharper consonant and a little tension in the lips will provide an elasticity that will produce a quasi-*staccato* without interfering with the flow of air. Play lighter in the rapid articulations for the pressures of a *fortissimo* are apt to slow and tongue-tie the performer. In that intermediate tempo, too fast for single and too slow for double, use a pairing of each, as in "*doodoo doogoo.*"

Staccatos are probably the most frequently misunderstood markings and are often used promiscuously by editors. The dot above the note theoretically subtracts half the value, but this is a broad generalization. There are perhaps dozens of varieties of *staccato* depending upon the context of the music. In the slower tempos these staccatos are realized by a small, articulated pulse or kick of the diaphragm, which activates a small bullet of air. They must sound short but still have a ring to the tone after the release. The shortness of sound must travel through the separation much as a struck bell or a vibrated *pizzacato* reverberates through the space between the notes. When the speed becomes too great for these individual diaphragmatic jabs, be sure that the diaphragm supports the series. Marcel Tabuteau used to advise his pupils to "articulate your wind, but do not wind your articulations."

For the inside articulations found in the pattern (♪♫), anticipate the inside note, for the tongue is mechanically inclined to be late in reaching it. Do likewise with the inside running couplets in the figuration (♫♫♫), which can be difficult in a fast tempo. As a corrective therapy, change the rhythm, and practice in a 32nd and dotted 16th rhythm—e.g.,

It is very difficult to articulate the notes below the low G with any degree of certainty, but the discreet opening and snapping of the G key (fingering the right hand in the meantime) at the exact instant the note is tongued somehow starts the air column vibrating and helps achieve a clean attack.

Articulation is precisely what the word implies: an attempt to make clear what the composer intends in the way of articulate communication. Use the same care and introspection that an actor would take in bringing to life a soliloquy of Hamlet.

FINGER TECHNIQUE

In addition to its more graceful, lyrical assignments, the flute through the centuries has been somewhat type-cast as the acrobat of the woodwinds. Whenever the composer orchestrates himself into an elaborate bird call or an extravagant technical situation, he almost instinctively turns to the flute for these flying-trapeze figurations. To survive in this world of gymnastics, the flutist must be equipped with a formidable agility and dexterity of the fingers. In spite of the differences in endowment and aptitude, the instrumentalist, with patience and determination, can do almost anything with his fingers. Although there is a kind of onerous drill and routine required, it should be remembered that the professional athlete is likewise involved in the same repetitive situation of calisthenics. This practice and discipline is best done in the early, formative years of youth, for in later years the learning processes are slowed and the reflexes less amenable to conditioning. Older students can never quite recapture that effortless, rippling facility that might have been acquired in the early teens. Finger technique refined early in study is, so to speak, money in the bank.

All technique begins with finger position, a position that permits the maximum efficiency with the minimum of effort and movement. The effort can be measured in ounces, and the movement in eighths of an inch. Fingers should be aligned directly, evenly and closely over the key cups. Any discrepancy in the height of the fingers over the keys results in a fractional sacrifice of time and unevenness in execution. A vertical thumb in the left hand locks in the functional wrist pronation. Slightly curved (rather than crabbed, tippy-toe) fingers are recommended for the right hand, since most of the control and action comes from the large knuckles. Support the flute with the right hand thumb in order to avoid too much bracing pressure on the right little finger, which can cramp the flexibility.

In terms of sheer velocity, it is quite possible to play at a rate of approximately a thousand notes per minute, almost too fast for the ear to apprehend except as swirls of notes. (Curiously, these swirls will sound faster if the notes are evenly distributed rather than faked through as a smear of sound.) Even though at this speed we are dealing with fractions of seconds, fluid finger technique depends on what transpires during that micro-second of finger movement. Although usually unobserved or ignored, something does happen to the sound, however transient, when a key is opened or closed. It is the performer's job to fill up this space with musical sound.

Where controlled single finger action is concerned, there is no problem providing that the air support is not affected by what our fingers are doing. But in the more clumsy exchanges and in the knarred cross and fork fingerings, the situation is complicated by an intricate synchronization of digital activity. Obviously, the greater the number of fingers involved, the greater the difficulty and the larger the margin for error and disturbance of sound. The second octave C-D, for instance, requires an extremely complex coordination of seven fingers and a thumb (an exchange that can be simplified by anticipating the D with the second and third fingers of the right hand while playing the C, and vice versa). Other changes, such as the third octave E-F, produce an inevitable clank which should be reduced to a minimum by diligent and attentive practice. The break involved in the three E-F♯ fingerings can be softened by lingering ever so slightly with the middle finger in moving to the F♯ and, conversely, by anticipating momentarily with the same finger in returning to the E.

These are but a few examples of the intricate finger changes that plague the flutist, and the implication, of course, is to isolate the difficulties and concentrate practice on the more complicated patterns. Practice them in slow motion, listening critically with a magnifying glass, so to speak, with the ear. Alternate them using various rhythms and proceed slowly to quasitrill or tremolo exercises. Be on guard rhythmically for, in spite of best intentions, the easy fingerings will tend to run and the difficult to drag. Equalize the two. Where there is a choice, a more difficult fingering will sometimes control a rushing situation.

Practice also what is most immediately useful. For example, a disproportionate amount of music is made up of scale and arpeggio passages. Since scales are almost exclusively made up of minor and major seconds and the arpeggios of thirds and fourths, concentrate on these. The Taffanel-Gaubert *Daily Exercise* calisthenics catalogue these basic formulas very well and constitute a bible of technique for the conscientious flutist. The numerous and assorted etudes, frequently deplored by the student, are also essential. It is conceivable that through practicing enough melodic and harmonic patterns, we program them into a subconscious reservoir of technique so that we do not really have to read new music, but rather to recognize and call up what we have already played and perfected.

Thoughtful repetition is the key to facility. Isolate the stumbling block in troublesome passages, superimpose repeat marks around them, and make exercises out of them. Attention given to finger action by the flutist is comparable to the consideration string players give to the fretting of the strings. Tempo and style can determine the character of finger movement required, and here again we are concerned with what happens in that critical, split second of change. Slow, *legato* finger action to stretch and enhance the intervals supplies an elasticity appropriate to the *lentos* and *adagios*, while a crisp, brittle finger articulation contributes a bright, sparkling *con brio* character to the fast *allegros* and *prestos*.

The tricky slides made by the little finger in the foot-joint action (C-Eb, C-E, etc.) can be facilitated by discreetly lubricating the finger with a little skin oil from the crease in the nose. The difficult interval break from high A ($G^\sharp$ to E) can be assured by lifting the right hand little finger and closing instantaneously as the E sounds.

Fingering charts together with the alternative fingerings for the spidery problem passages are available and should be used. Many seemingly impossible combinations can be solved by carefully substituting an harmonic fingering in a strategic spot. Dogged patience, time and drill will do the rest. Frequently, just thinking in terms of groups of notes and their rhythmic and harmonic resolutions will eliminate the self-conscious block in a difficult running figuration and keep them from sounding fingery.

The metronome is the instrumentalist's best friend and a surrogate teacher at his side. Besides supplying an unyielding discipline, it also provides a reassuring measure of progress.

In the final analysis, it is the acute and analytical listening that provides the direction toward a clean and facile technique.

Part II

Phrasing

SONG VS. DANCE ELEMENTS

All too often our musical instruction is preoccupied with the literal reproduction of notation, with explicit attention directed to the precise tempo, rhythmic and dynamic markings—plus, perhaps, accents placed on the strong beats to demonstrate that the performer has a good sense of rhythm. Or, frequently, the big consideration is to fill up all the notes with ravishing sound. While quite an accomplishment in itself, all this can never amount to more than a sophisticated craft of reproduction, a kind of xeroxing in sound of the notation. The visual division of music into measure units and barred beat groups contributes to this static framing of the music.

On the other hand, music, by its very nature, is sound in motion and is immediately involved with the progression of time. Far from being a simple, calculated division of time, the rhythmic energy, voice leading and harmonic progressions should be so disposed as to shape and punctuate this time sequence into meaningful, musical language. As with any language, the same concerns with grammar and syntax prevail. There must be a logical plan of continuity and horizontal organization of the materials, for music must always move and travel coherently.

Marcel Tabuteau, the eminent former oboist of the Philadelphia Orchestra, was fond of defining music in more philosophical terms as the "friction between space and time"—that is to say, an interplay of tensions between the freedom of the horizontal line (space) and the vertical discipline of the rhythm (time). Or, more simply, the interrelationships of the song and dance elements present to some degree in all music. The metrical rhythm acts as a musical gravity to hold the song elements in check, and, in the process, creates an interaction of tension and resolution impulses that make up the physical and emotional communications of music.

PHRASE GROUPINGS

As noted earlier, the metrical rhythms of music (basically two and three) are frequently emphasized in performance by placing dynamic accents on the primary beats. William Kincaid, on the other hand, considered these beat notes as points of arrival, as the result of what happened *before* the beat was reached. The character of the beat was conditioned by *how* it was reached. Normally, the harmonic changes occur on the strong beats of the measure, but there are also melodic and rhythmic sequences which move to the beat. These beats are terminations rather than beginnings of phrases; they are the resultants of a progression, not the start of a phrase.

All this is quite basic and natural and is directly related to our environmental and biological lives. We are surrounded by such rhythms both in nature (the ebb and flow of the sea, the action of pendulums) and in our own bodies (the beats of the heart, the rhythms of respiration). As a simple analogy, our steps are like strong primary beats of music, and the character of each step is determined by how we move into it, whether it be by gliding, marching, striding, lunging, skipping or running.[1] The weight and pressure of the step is conditioned by what we do between the steps, producing a

[1]The earth's gravity is involved not only in the up and down energy impulses of walking but also many other bodily motions. It is provocative to speculate whether or not rhythm and music as we know them could have evolved in the weightlessness of space.

natural inevitability at these points of arrival. They are resultants rather than beginnings of movement. Conducting, as another example, is almost entirely physical imagery, for here the description of the beat is conditioned by what the conductor does *between* and *before* the beats. In summary, rhythm is not superimposed with dynamic accents but rather evolves from the interior progressions to the beat.

The measuring and barring of our notation, it must be remembered, is a reading convenience, but the consequent visual blocking of the notes into beat groups works against the flow of the musical line. Normally (unless the impulse implies a resolution), an isolated couplet, triplet, quadruplet or sextolet (illustration a) is unfinished and incomplete, like having a foot in the air with no place to put it:

(a)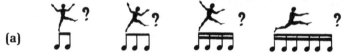

These figurations ask a question and resolve nothing unless they move on to the next beat (illustration b). In other words, it takes three notes to distinguish a couplet, four for a triplet, five for a quadruplet and seven for a sextolet:

(b)

Following these considerations, William Kincaid considered all beat notes as a kind of point of balance and called them "finishing notes." To indicate the resolution movement, he devised a system of phrase groupings, consisting of a bracketing of related notes in a kind of family relationship, to show their identification with, and progression to, this finishing note. This is best illustrated in the running divisions of the quarter as follows:[1]

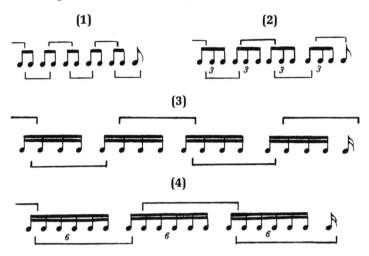

To control the spread and distribution of the sextolet, interior groupings are sometimes made as follows:

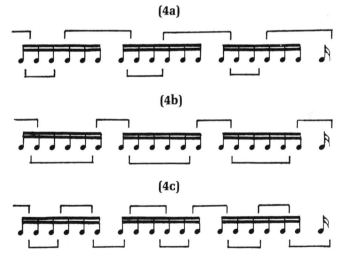

[1]Naturally, the same considerations apply to other units and combinations of the rhythm and, by extension, to entire measures as well:

As the brackets indicate, the first note of the figuration is always a finishing note, a note to set the tonality or a point of rhythm, the end of something preceding, even if imagined.[1] The real impulse and movement begins with the inside note and travels through the grouping by graduating the dynamics, articulations and intensities of each note in a symmetrical progression to the finishing note. All are carefully scaled so as to indicate the direction of the musical line.

This subtle grouping organization is perhaps better described in terms of a verbal analogy. The individual notes belong to each other and combine in the same sense that letters of the alphabet merge and take on a new relationship in syllables. Just as the intelligibility in language comes from the pronunciation of the syllable, so musical intelligibility comes from the pronunciation of the grouping as a coherent unit. Essentially, phrasing is the difference between spelling out note names or vocalizing them as a musical syllable. These syllabic units, by extension, combine to form word-motifs, phrases, sentences, etc.

As part of this group scaling, an inflection is supplied at the beginning of each grouping to show the direction and imply the resolution. This impulse is identical with the *up bow* feeling of a stringed instrument; the lifted part of the grouping

---

[1] Bach frequently omits the thesis and begins with the arsis. Schweitzer in his *Out of My Life and Thought* (italics mine) observed that: "It is characteristic of the structure of his periods that as a rule they do not start from an accent but *strive to reach one*. They are conceived as beginning with an upward beat. It must, further, be noticed that in Bach the accents of the lines of sound do not as a rule coincide with the natural accents of the bars, but advance side by side with those in a freedom of their own. From this *tension* between the accents of the line of sound and those of the bars comes the extraordinary rhythmical vitality of Bach's music." Albert Schweitzer, *Out of My Life and Thought* (Holt, Rinehart and Winston: New York, 1953), pg. 57.

is resolved on a *down bow* impulse at the end of the sequence:

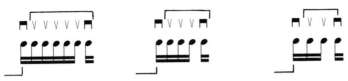

In this area, the winds have a great advantage over the strings in that they are not constricted by the mechanical considerations of bowing.

With his French love of logic and precision, Marcel Tabuteau preferred to describe this scaling of impulse and intensity more explicitly in terms of numbers. Each note was assigned a number indicating the degree of intensity and dynamic with which it was to be played. Any repetition of the same number (see illustration) implied a change of bow or impulse.[1] One of his great talents was the imaginative contouring and assigning of these numbers. As an example of his meticulous concern with scaling, he might have numbered a very simple passage as follows:

Or he might (the numbers are arbitrary) have shaped the opening *andante* of the Bach Sonata No. 4 for flute and keyboard as follows:

[1] My account of Tabuteau's numbering system is greatly over-simplified. For further details, procure the Marcel Tabuteau Memorial Album, *Art of the Oboe* (Stereo #1717, Coronet Recording Co.).

Obviously, the Tabuteau numbered sequences very closely parallel the Kincaid phrase groupings concept. In either case, do not mark the groupings or make them too obvious for they are simply subtly imposed undulations to and from the beat. Kincaid used to warn his students to "think the groupings, but don't do them." Make all nuances *within* the groupings. Greater liberties, more in the sense of a Chopin *rubato,* are similarly taken within the measure so that the metric frame is not distorted. Use the metronome as a discipline, but play *against* it. Playing *with* it is a mere, mechanical calculation. Tabuteau advised his students to "Ride the rhythm; don't let it ride you."

The groupings will facilitate reading, for most harmonic and melodic changes occur after the finishing note. They will also help to keep quadruplets from sounding like a pair of couplets, triplets from falling into a duple rhythm, sextuplets from dividing into pairs of triplets, etc. In running ensemble passages it is common practice to make the ensemble coincidence on the beat note; but it is the *second* note (first note of the phrase grouping) that is the control note. It determines the inflection and direction of the phrase. It is good ensemble practice to omit the beat note until the grouping is set.

In order to consolidate the feeling of the groupings and make them more instinctive, practice alternating them between teacher and pupil in scale and running passages, as indicated below:

LARGHETTO *ANDERSEN, Op. 33*

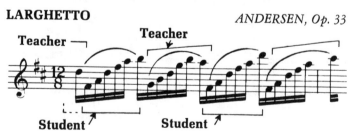

Normally, avoid the slurs that coincide with the groupings, for this erases the friction and the results become soapy.

Far from being a merely theoretical approach to music, these phrase groupings provide an effective tool and produce a natural flow in the musical line. They add an organization and shape to the line that supplies a continuity of musical ideas. In addition, they will furnish a subtle undercurrent of rhythm and impulse without the heavy-handed marking of beats, and add a strong rhythmic vitality because of the progressions to and from the beat.

LEGATO INTERVALS

Indispensable to the playing of a line of music or the spinning out of a beautiful *legato* phrase is the ability of a flutist to weave his tone through broken chords and disjunct intervals without interrupting the flow and line of sound. The flute alone among the wood winds has the *advantage* of having no octave key.[1] Because the flutist has to *produce* and not just finger the intervals, there is a natural, harmonic quality to these shifts of pitch. Much of the time he is working with the overtone series in the octave, fifth, fourth and third relationships so that, ideally, there is a natural kind of slippage from one note to another. This joining together of notes is difficult to describe, but it is comparable to the natural breaks of the human voice, the *portamento* of the French Horn as it glides from one partial to another, or the refined

---

[1] Naturally, there is a venting of holes to clear some intervals, particularly in the third octave, but basically the registration changes are accomplished with the air and the lips.

glissando that the violinists call the "Heifetz shift." The wood thrush has this liquid connection between notes of its call which supplies a haunting flute-like quality to its song.

For the flutist, all this demands a fine dexterity of the lips and a delicate manipulation of the air, but, more importantly, it requires a concentration of listening and an acute consciousness of what happens during those instantaneous shifts of intervals. Ordinarily the changes occur too quickly to be analyzed by the ear so they must be practiced in slow motion till the shifts become second nature.

To get back to essentials, each note of the flute, *irrespective of the dynamic,* must have a certain energy or speed of wind, relative to its position in the scale of the instrument, to produce a live, convincing sound. It is one thing to find the optimum placement for a single note but quite another to move from one pitch placement to another, bridging, in the meantime, this leap with sound. Intervals can be forced or simply fingered, but the musical solution is found in *preparing* the leap, whether up or down, on the preceding note by increasing or reducing the intensity of the first note to the relative intensity level of the second *before* making the change. It is much like taking an elevator or an escalator to a selected floor *before* moving off at the new level.

This technique is best illustrated in the following slow motion example of the octave shift where, in effect, a musical ramp of intensity is constructed between the notes. Wind velocity is slowly increased (a) from, say, ten to twenty miles per hour by a gradual compression of the lips and added support from the diaphragm. At the critical moment a deft, compressive shift of the lips (forward) and change in air direction (up) will produce a musical glide to the top octave.

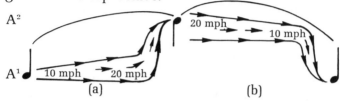

The action is reversed in the descending octave leap (b). However, due to the lack of an octave key, this break down is more difficult to execute and requires the addition of a rather special technique. In general, the intensity on the top octave is slowly reduced by gradually relaxing the lips and diaphragmatic support and at the last moment the embouchure shift (lips back, air angled down) is made so that the octave settles into the fundamental and is gripped as it sounds. In order to expedite this stubborn transition during the embouchure shift, the lips are almost simultaneously opened and closed in a minute nibble—a kind of musical sleight of hand, like dropping the sound and instantly catching it on a cushion of air.

Much of this becomes a kinesthetic sensation and probably is best described in terms of physical analogies. Interval slurs resemble the execution of a swan dive from the preparatory, springboard generation of energy to the soaring glide of the descent. Or they are like the distribution of energies in the snap, catch and extension calisthentics of the weight lifter (see illustration).

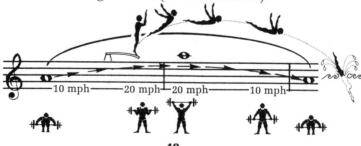

This same procedure applies to all intervals, no matter how small or large. The degree of embouchure shift is subtly adjusted to the size of the interval. Lean on the lower notes as though you were pressing them into the upper and diminish on the upper notes to float them into the lower. *In each case the intensity is raised or lowered on the preceding note to the relative intensity of the second.* It's sometimes helpful to imagine playing the intensities of the intermediate notes between the interval on the previous note. Get the note to which you are slurring in the lip before playing it so that the intervals evolve into one another. Always fill the space between the notes with supported breath and sound. Keep the intensity curves convex and avoid the scoops and slurps of a bad vocalist.

Tabuteau suggested that "octaves should be desired," and it is precisely this expectation of change, evoked by the preparation, that communicates your intentions to your audience and, to an extent, invites their sympathetic participation in your performance.

In the more rapid exchanges the flutist needs instant compressions and decompressions of air, instant speeds of wind. The time required for a snap of the fingers is approximately 1/10th of a second. Certainly the lips are just as sensitive and responsive, so that great flexibility is possible in minute fractions of the second. Consequently, do not set the lips into a fixed embouchure position but keep them flexible.

Ideally, what is accomplished by all this is a liquid continuity and resonance that leaves one note sounding while another is being produced, an almost reverberated overlapping that can add an harmonic character to the melodic line of a single voiced instrument.

LINE

As the word implies, line is the final shaping of the breath into meaningful trajectories of sound. It is a conscious, superimposed pattern of sound which is impelled by the rhythm and impulses of the phrase groupings. Line evolves in terms of dynamics, intensity and color.

Regardless of the size of the musical unit, an appropriate line of breath is first determined:

Once the line is established, the notes are placed on it:

The contour of this line is arbitrary (subjective judgments based on harmonic, melodic and rhythmic progressions), and may assume as many forms as there are line drawings or styles of music:

 etc.

However, a succession of totally symmetric lines would, of course, become intolerably bland without the addition of grammatical inflections which permit the music to make assertions, to insinuate, to ask questions, to exclaim, to interject, etc. So, since the overall shape of a musical period or section involves the organization of smaller motif or phrase lines (lines within lines), these larger lines are punctuated (internally and externally) with all the inflections of speech—i.e., the musical equivalents of commas, hyphens, colons, question marks, exclamation marks, parentheses, etc.:

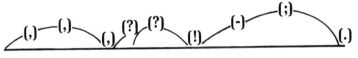

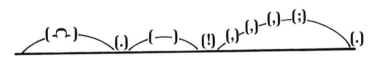

Detached articulations fit this concept of line; they are simply the separation of the flow of air into impulses placed on the line. Make sure that these releases of impulses do not interrupt, but rather (like little arrows of sound) imply the continuation and direction of the line:

To establish a good line of continuity, it is a good procedure to slur tongued passages first and then simply articulate the slur-breath line.

Illustrated below is an intentionally obvious example (again, Andersen, *Etude No. 5*, Op. 33) of how the line of a simple phrase evolves:

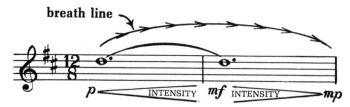

Breath line established and contoured over a single note.

Skeletal notes placed on same breath line; each note travels toward and evolves into the next.

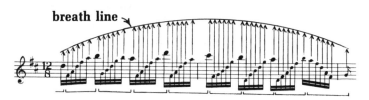

Interior decoration of skeletal notes incorporated into breath line. (Impulses of the phrase groupings reinforce the configurations of the line.)

In extended lines with complicated figurations, it is obviously impossible, what with the limitations in the expressive range of the instrument, to keep making rising and falling lines indefinitely. Consequently, small nuances (delicately graduated within the phrase groupings and moving to the line) are frequently made, as illustrated below:

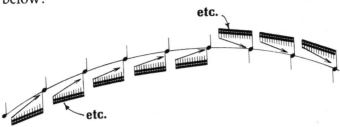

I hope these diagrams will illustrate the control and concern that goes into scaling the various stresses and relaxations of music so that these tensions and resolutions are prepared and anticipated. Rather than willy-nilly following the profiles of the melodic line, superimpose a planned pattern. Tell the notes what to do, not vice versa, so that all intervals and figurations conform to, rather than determine the line. Take the scoops out of *crescendos* and *diminuendos*—think of them as convex rather than concave curves. Concentrate on playing between the notes, over and through the bar lines, and distribute the breath in a constant stream with no interruptions so that the progression of the line is not lost. Music, no matter how bad, is never static so you must always move and travel in your playing. See, also, that you move on the sustained notes. Mold the tone and make it travel by means of changes in intensity, volume and color. Avoid phrasing exclusively in terms of volume.

As indicated earlier, the profile of a line is arbitrary. The important consideration is not having the *right* plan, but having *a* plan. It is possible, through accumulated experience and certain intuitive expectations, to play off the top of your head, but the conscientious musician will explore a phrase, tilting it sideways, backwards and upside down, till he selects the right option for himself and for the music, much as an actor will probe into the characterization of a Shakespearean line before settling on his particular inflection, accent or gesture.

Line can be as simple or as fussy as the music indicates. In searching for the profile, it is advisable to eliminate the musical embroidery and look for the significant skeletal notes, whose position and harmonic weight will outline the contour. Frequently after some examination, an ornate passage will be found to be based on a simple scale or triad progression whose notes will pinpoint the schematic design of the line. Too often a line, like an over-dressed woman, is overly decorated with effects and detail which obscures the basic structure. Frequently, the greatest challenge is to play music simply and severely.

The historical periods with their stylistic considerations are important too and condition the shape and character of the line. In very general terms, the Classical period (Haydn) with its clean, lean lines is better done simply. The *roulade* configurations of the rococo style (Mozart) suggest more decorative accommodations. Beethoven, with his revolutionary expostulations, indicates a more literal, dynamic approach. The Romantics (Tschaikowsky, Brahms) require coloristic considerations. The late Romantics (Strauss, Mahler) with their emotional erruptions and interjections demand a more elaborate punctuation, while the Impressionists (Debussy, Ravel) imply a diffused focus and limpid sound. Each period has a style and a color, and each movement of a work within the style has its own individual character. The performer must, so to speak, set the stage for each work to be played.

Since, more often than not, phrases resolve on the down impulse (strong beats of the measure), do not breathe between up and down impulses, but always after the finishing note (between phrase groupings) even though it may mean sometimes breaking a slur. Avoid bar breathing like sin, unless:

1. the phrase ends on a relatively long note;

2. the same note or chord is repeated across the bar line;

3. or on those occasions when the phrase definitely ends within the bar line.

To preserve the proportion of a line, avoid accenting or pressing leading tones into the tonic, particularly in cadences where you most often find the beautiful descending lines. The leading tones have enough harmonic weight by themselves without the added pressure.

Don't be mechanical in playing accompanying figures. The most banal "Ump-pa-pa" accompaniment can take on significance if it is related, dynamically and expressively, to the progression of a melodic line. In such ensemble situations, rehearse the accompanying patterns separately with one ear tuned to the line of the leading voice.

Happily, there is no *one definitive* solution to a phrasing problem; rather, there are *several definitive* solutions with the validity of each depending upon the personal frame of reference and the conviction with which it is executed.

Part III
Some Elements of Musical Execution

RHYTHM

To distribute the values of odd numbered series of notes (e.g., triplets, quintuplets, septuplets) evenly, think of balancing them on the middle note:

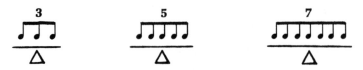

Prepare your subdivisions by calculating them on a preceding note, but, instead of thinking ♪♪♪♪♪♪ / 1 2 3 4 5 6, as in the case of sextuplets, start with the unit number of the distribution and count forward to the resolution on the next beat—i.e., ♪♪♪♪♪♪ ♩ / 6 1 2 3 4 5 6. Use this counting method for all subdivisions and you will never run out of space or have any left over:

♪♪♪ ♩   ♪♪♪♪ ♩   ♪♪♪♪♪ ♩
3 1 2 3   4 1 2 3 4   5 1 2 3 4 5

In a group of two or more moving notes, position the first note well. It is better to play the first note of a group too long, rather than too short.

In florid swirls, pick out certain pivotal notes within the figurations to move to and regulate the distribution of the notes. The runs, because of the controlled spread of note values, will sound *faster* than a virtuostic splash of notes and will prevent rushing to the next beat. (If you arrive early, there is no way to compensate.) For example, in a twelve note run you could position the pivotal notes as follows: (The impulses are different in each instance and depend somewhat upon the subdivision of the accompanying rhythm.)

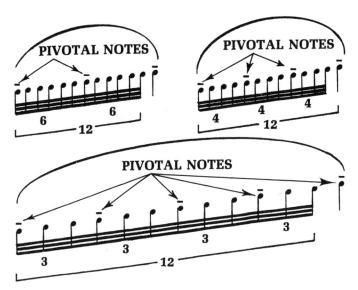

In rhapsodic, cadenza-like passages, it is possible to group the running notes into progressively larger (or smaller) units to provide built-in *rubatos, accelerandos* and *rallentandos* within the beat unit. Septuplets, for instance, could be grouped into:

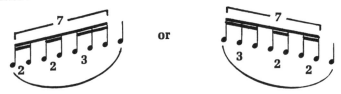

Or a fifteen note flourish can be grouped:

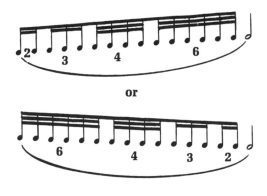

Anticipate and stress all syncopated notes slightly, in many cases with a color and not a dynamic accent. But do not mark the beat within the syncopation; feed the air toward the pulse instead.

Cross rhythms are not the segregation of two rhythms but rather their interaction, producing a push-pull of forces with neither of the rhythms dominating, much like the interaction of opposing linemen on a football team:

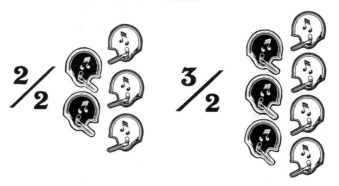

Practice them *against* the metronome (2 against 3, 3 against 4, etc.) till they are felt naturally and not as the calculated groupings of the common denominators. Conductors, for their own convenience, too often conduct the cross rhythm, thus eliminating the friction and fun of playing against the fundamental beat.

When you have couplets following triplets (or vice versa), subtly exaggerate the rhythms so as to maintain the identity of each. The audience should be able to identify the rhythmic figure from the performer's inflections.

Rapidly slurred octaves more often than not sound uneven because of the natural tendency of the instrument to break into the upper octave prematurely ♪♪♪. To counteract and correct the tendency, reverse the rhythm and practice them as follows: ♪♪♪ . Play them almost this way and they will *sound* even.

TEMPOS

Follow the example of good jazz musicians and mentally "kick-off" the rhythmic meter before starting a composition. Too often, beginning tempos are tentative and not consolidated until half way through the second or third measure.

Give attention to the *numerators* in the signature of the rhythmic markings: $\frac{2}{4}$ $\frac{4}{8}$ $\frac{3}{2}$ $\frac{6}{4}$ etc., and see to it that the pulses are properly observed, even though they do not, necessarily, coincide with the conducting tempo. Frequently, an *alla breve* (¢) is conducted in four, but the playing should reflect the basic meter of two. Search for the fundamental pulse in other meters and observe it in your performance to avoid sounding subdivided in your playing.

A skillful composer will arrange his tempo changes much as an accomplished playwright will organize the timing of a good scenario. The scenario of the music evolves through a variety of movements anticipated by tempo accommodations. An *accelerando* may lead into an *allegro,* and a *rallentando* can set the stage for an *adagio,* or a *subito presto* may interject the excitement of a new episode and a *meno,* the resolution of the same excitement. Search for the logic behind the evolution of the musical setting and relate the parts to the whole.

Metronomic markings are relative, and there is probably no such thing as *a* definitive tempo for any specific composition; rather there are several, the validity of each depending upon the style and conviction of the performance. Many great composers, Beethoven and Wagner included, have had second thoughts about assigning specific metronomic markings to their works. Each conductor has his own reference, and each performer has his own technical facility, individual temperament, personalized conception of the style, and a musical metabolism all of his own. Your "fast" is not necessarily my "fast" and my heart may not beat in the same 3/4 time as yours, so we cannot be too categorical in matters of time. The old saying "Tempo is determined by the blackest (busiest) part of the music" is axiomatic. The wise performer will use this area as a gauge in determining the surrounding and related tempos.

Do not become too sentimental with *ritards, rallentandos* and *calandos*. They are conventionally used in three ways:

1. expressively, to dwell over the emotional value of a high point in a phrase line;
2. transitionally, to introduce or lead into a change of tempo;
3. structurally, to define the closing of a section.

Discriminate between the functions and apply accordingly. There are times for extravagances (characteristic music) and times for austerity (the more classical frame of reference). At any rate, avoid the stop-and-go effects induced by the indiscriminate use of *ritards*. It is possible to give the indication of a relaxation by starting with the *ritard* impulse and then immediately progressing a tempo. It implies the inflection without actually executing it. At other times a simple broadening of the line accomplishes the same effect. Again, "think don't do it."

Rubato, literally, is "stolen time" except that it is a Robin Hood variety of stealing in which the stolen goods have to be redistributed. Consequently, make the *rubatos* within the phrase groupings, or, in more extravagant situations, within the measure so that the frame of each unit remains intact.

Pick-ups are normally played in the tempo of the resolving section, even though they may be positioned in a movement of a different tempo.

In rapid solo passages, the accompaniment should *seem* to hold you back giving the impression of activity and speed in the solo line. Conversely, in the slow solo movements the accompaniment should *seem* to pull ahead. Without this friction, the rapid passages are liable to run and the slow to drag.

BREATHING POINTS

All music must breathe. The resourceful wind player will so plan his necessary breathing points that they work to his advantage in punctuating his musical line.

Correct breathing leaves the note sounding *while* you breathe. The sound seems to coast through the separation and, to an extent, disguises the abruptness of the break in the line. Learn to breathe out on the gentle releases (like blowing out a candle) so that the sound is tapered off, keeping the air moving even after the sound has evaporated. To catch a fast breath, imitate the rapid, almost simultaneous, in-out action of a bellows. The diaphragm clears the lungs of air and, almost in the same instant, recovers a fresh breath. (It is important to get rid of the stale air as well as to replenish the lungs with a fresh supply of oxygen.) This technique becomes automatic with practice.

Always breathe soon enough and on a point of rhythm. Because of an honest attempt to give full value to the release note, wind players are chronically late on the following entrance. Adjust by discreetly stealing breath time from the release note. Give attention to the *manner* of the release (lifted, feathered, skipping, abrupt, etc.) which is as much an ingredient of musical punctuation as the attack. (Make sure that the end of the note is always left open and never dampened by any action of the tongue or lips.) There are times, again for reasons of punctuation, when you must give the impression of a breath even though it is not necessary or desirable; in these circumstances learn to *simulate* the impulse of a breath.

Avoid breathing before large intervals. Play through them instead. The wide leaps are generally the more expressive intervals, and the performing of them should communicate the expressive exertion involved in their production. When possible, stretch the wide intervals so that the space between them is filled with sound. Make a slight *rubato* and compensate later.

Playing long, sustained passages is not a matter of vital breath capacity but rather one of breath control. In order to stretch the air over a long phrase, work backwards from the high point so that the dynamics can be scaled and the breath distributed toward the climax.

In some slower, articulated passages it is possible to maintain a long line by pumping up your lungs with little "snifters" taken through the nose and between the tonguings.

Remind yourself to breathe normally when nervous. Shallow breathing, as well as chest heaving (which can lead to hyperventilation), will only affect the heart activity and consequently increase the anxiety.

DYNAMICS

Do not be too literal in observing dynamic markings. More often than not they are positioned throughout a phrase to pin-point the contour of the line. Consequently, work backwards from the *fortissimos* and *pianissimos* to determine how they are to be reached. Similarly, prepare the accents, *sforzandos*, etc. Like the bodily action that anticipates a lunge or a stab, the impulse that *generates* the musical gesture (like the threat of a clenched fist) is just as important, and sometimes as effective, as the gesture itself.

Discriminate between the dynamic and expressive accents. The expressive are better accomplished with a quick vibrato, a change of color, a minute *tenuto*—or all three.

In passages which have an echo-like dynamic opposition (f____/p____), maintain the *forte* up to the moment of the *piano* so that the contrast is well defined. In one of his favorite analogies, Tabuteau compared the *fp* to the action of a bird flying sixty miles per hour, then lighting on a wire without jarring it. In many circumstances a small breath or hesitation is appropriate before an extreme dynamic change.

Dynamics are relative. The emotional impact of a performer's *fortissimo* is directly related to the level and delicacy of his *pianissimo*. The larger American auditoriums, however, require a wider dynamic range than is necessary or sufficient for small recital halls.

The performer is always a victim of his own presence and is no better able to judge the sound of his own instrument than he is to judge the sound of his own voice. Yet, as a kind of public speaker, he must use a projected quality which is not always as dulcet as he would like it to be at close range. Only through experience (and the advice of others) does he learn that there must be small exaggerations in performance in order to fill up the space between performer and audience. Dynamics and intensities are like an actor's make-up. The same make-up which looks grotesque at close range appears natural from the vantage of the fifteenth row in the audience. The performer must, so to speak, position himself mentally in the first balcony and listen back to himself.

FAKE FINGERING

Do not be a purist in the sense of never resorting to any type of harmonic, trill or so-called fake fingering. There is nothing so chaste or uncompromising about some of the pure fingerings to begin with, and frequently the character of the music demands a lightness and facility that can only be accomplished with the fake fingerings. Used with discretion, they are often the more *musical* solution to the playing of an otherwise clumsy handful of notes.

ORNAMENTS

Grace notes are decorative and, like the tasteful use of jewelry, should enhance rather than distract. They are executed delicately and should be resolved rhythmically and dynamically on the principal note with a caressing impulse of the air. Use trill fingerings for the graces where possible, not because they are easier, but because of the lightness obtained from the simplified key action. Never accent or play the grace louder than the principal note; the musical gesture is always one of resolution. The speed of the execution should be related to the context of the movement—gentle, for instance, in an *adagio* and snappy in a *scherzo*. Graces under a slur and coming just before a relatively strong beat of the measure may be softly touched with the tongue.

The problems of playing baroque ornaments and *appoggiaturas* (long, short, before the beat, on the beat, etc.) are better left to the discriminating ear than to the mind. As more and more information is accumulated regarding the performing conventions of the early periods, there seems to be less and less consensus on specific applications. Explore the practices of these periods but do not be intimidated by the musicologists. It is better to avoid a calculated ornament that cannot be performed with taste and conviction. Mozart *appoggiaturas* generally can be played short if they are below the principal note and long if above, not because of any theoretical rule but simply because they sound better that way.

Unless explicitly indicated, do not mark the trills in a line of sound. The trilling itself is a kind of accent. Avoid the alarmclock sort of reaction to the trill sign and always relate the speed of the trill to the tempo and character of the movement, sometimes graduating the flutter of the trill to indicate the progression of the line. Be on guard to tune and match the quality of the two trilled notes.

Often, particularly in cadences, trills are terminated by pausing momentarily on a point of rhythm (frequently the second half of the trilled note), before resolving. In playing these trills make one more turn than you think you should before pausing. This makes the termination sound less thumpy and calculated.

COUPLETS

When articulation forms the interior decoration of a line, do not let the tongued details interfere with the essential shape and design of the phrase. For example, the second note of slurred couplets, for some reason, is often clipped, producing a scalloping of the line:

Unless specifically indicated, play these second notes broadly to maintain the continuity and line of sound.

MEMORIZATION

Avoid finger memorizing. A small fumble will shatter the progression and let you down in performance. Instead, vocalize the progressions and *memorize the intervals*, being on the lookout for melodic and harmonic sequences that will guide you through the thicket of modifying notes. It is a habit that improves with use, and the confidence for doing it is best established in the early, formative years of study. At least memorize the difficult, thorny passages in solo and ensemble passages. In many instances the reading difficulty of a busy notation can be more of a distraction than a cue. To test your memorization, try transposing an etude or solo to a different key by ear.

ENSEMBLE

Ensemble playing requires a perfect understanding between performers, for the moment you begin to listen for note changes, it is too late! Take your dynamic levels from the other instruments and, to an extent, try to match their qualities so as to maintain the line as the theme is tossed from instrument to instrument.

Use distance to determine the balance. Have someone go outside the studio and close the door to judge.

Part IV
A Final Word

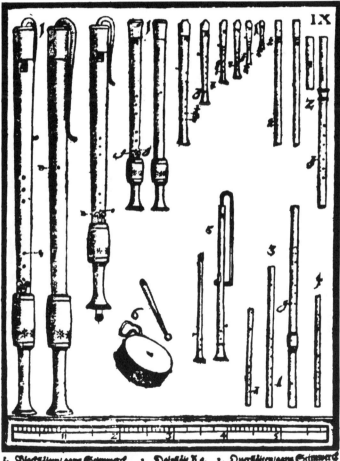

THE FLUTE REPERTOIRE

The flute repertoire is so immense that the eyes glaze and the mind boggles when groping through the multiple choices available in assembling recital programs. In order to reduce your library to practical and manageable proportions, cross-index it under the following categories:

    UNACCOMPANIED SOLOS
    SOLOS WITH ACCOMPANIMENT
    SONATAS
    CONCERTOS
    CONCERTINAS
    SONATINAS
    SUITES
    ENSEMBLES 2 3 4 5 6 etc.

Go to the original edition wherever possible and maintain a healthy suspicion of all edited markings, particularly in the instance of early works where such indications were non-existent or at an absolute minimum. Today there are literally editions-of-editions being released and, by the time the music reaches you, it has passed through the hands of several editors, each of whom can be a little cavalier and promiscuous about superimposing tempo, articulation, ornamentation, dynamic and stylistic indications. You as the performer, with some investigation and research, have as much right to make the adjustments as they.

When studying a composition, work from the cue line of the accompanying part, not only to relate the two parts but to check for any discrepencies. It would appear that in many instances the solo part has been extracted from this cue line and that frequent errors and omissions occur in the printing process.

Searching for a valid interpretation is very similar to the deductive reasoning process used in solving a detective story. Get out your magnifying glass and be a Sherlock Holmes, searching out all the clues and circumstantial evidence—title, signature, pulse, dynamics, form, period, stylistic clues and biographical data on the composer himself. Only after all this available evidence is accumulated and digested are you in a position to make a deduction or an educated guess as to the composer's motives, style and meaning.

POSTLUDE

Much of the material I have assembled here represents a kind of musical etiquette, a sort of "Robert's Rules of Musical Order." However, there is another ineffable element that cannot be included in these notes because it defies analysis, imitation and description. It is the element of freedom (immeasurable though it may be) inherent in almost everything we play. Mozart himself, for example, speaks of playing against the beat.[1] Rules are made to be bent, and even bad taste, in the right circumstance, can be good taste.

The senior members of the Philadelphia Orchestra when recalling the great performances of the century speak nostalgically and reverently of that rare and elusive quality of an artist which they

[1] . . . "The correctness of my time astonishes them all. The tempo *rubato* in an adagio with the left hand keeping strict time was quite beyond their comprehension. They always follow with the left hand." (Mozart to his Father, Augsburg, Aug. 24, 1777.)

choose to call "fantasy." They mean that these artists, knowing all the rules, do something so subtle in terms of an unexpected twist of a phrase, a subliminal hesitation, a shimmer of color, a manipulation of the rhythm, a deft shift of impulse or a shiver of anticipation that it is impossible to capture it in words. Yet, they all weave an enchantment into their performances that stops your heart and catches your breath. Kincaid belonged among these men, and the magic of his artistry lingers in the ears of those who remember.

If this can be learned, it is best done by astute listening to the great performing artists of the past and present and by exposing one's nerve endings to the immense variety of nature and life. Music can be a kind of tonal and physical recreation and should mirror the sheer joy of involvement and movement in life itself.

An informal concert by the Philadelphia Orchestra, Leopold Stokowski conducting, at the Broad Street Station of the Pennsylvania Railroad, April 27, 1952. The Orchestra was leaving on a tour of New England. Flutists are (l. to r.) Robert Cole, John Krell, Kenton Terry, and William Kincaid.

Appendixes

A. FACTORS IN TONE PRODUCTION

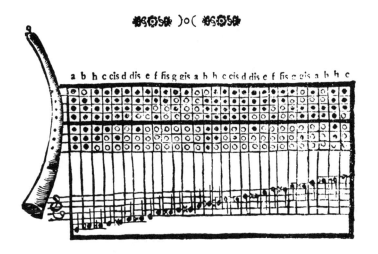

Sooner or later all flutists graduate from the supervision of their teachers and are discharged from all the flute clinics. They are then dependent on their own resources and must doctor their own flute maladies.

In a graphic shorthand manner, the following is an attempt to isolate all those factors of tone production (diaphragm, coverage, flow of air, direction of air, resonance) that the flutist can physically control or alter. It is hoped that these little cartoons may be helpful to the flutist in analyzing and conditioning his sound.

Obviously there is more than one way to play the flute and my indications are intended simply as suggestions. Some flutists may prefer to play with a more open embouchure hole or have other means of altering directions of the air, etc.

FACTORS IN TONE PRODUCTION

I. Diaphragm

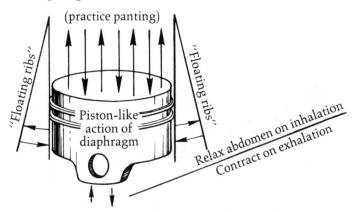

II. Coverage of Embouchure Hole

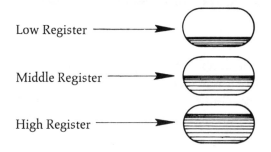

III. Direction of Air Stream

1. Up-Down

    (Use pivot of jaw)

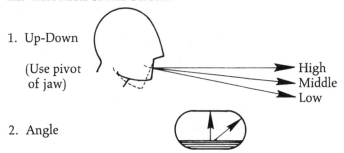

2. Angle

3. Tilt of head joint - slightly in

III. Flow of Wind

1. Amount of wind (volume)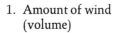

2. Speed of wind (intensity)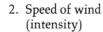

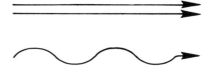

3. Shape of wind

   a) width of stream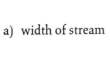

   b) degree of opening (grip)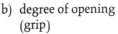

   c) length of lip tube (nozzle)

   d) shape of mouth (funnel)

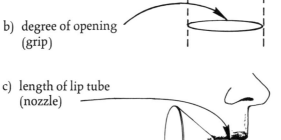

IV. Resonance

1. Mouth, tongue (vowel sounds)

2. Open throat (yawn)

3. Rib cage (extended up & out)

   (Like speaker cabinet)

B. DAILY PRACTICE ROUTINES AND MATERIALS

Kincaid in his studio.

I. Daily Practice Routines

The serious flute student should establish a firm schedule of practice—preferably two hours in the morning and two in the afternoon with little breaks in between to rest the lip and maintain the concentration.

Search out a studio that is not too live or too dead acoustically; the first will flatter your sound and deceive you, while the second is just too humiliating and encourages forcing. Adjust the acoustics by hanging drapes, opening windows, etc. —anything to break up the opposing wall reflections of sound.

See to it that the practice is balanced without any one crash program on fingers, articulation or tone; sometimes one works to the disadvantage of the other. Establish a well adjusted distribution of effort so that all the facets of playing are covered daily. The following routine (again in shorthand form) is suggested:

1. Flageolett (whistle) tones:
a) play up and down on the harmonic series.
b) select one and sustain for 10 seconds.
c) play tunes on 3rd octave fingerings.

2. Sustained tones: (10 counts at 1 = 60 — no vibrato) — crescendo - diminuendo patterns — fade-ins and fade-outs — modulations of intensity and color — Moyse, *De La Sonorité*, etc.

3. Intervals: Slow octaves, 3rds, 4ths, 5ths, 6ths, 7ths, etc. — Taffanel-Gaubert interval patterns from *Exercices Journaliers*, — Maquarre, *Daily Exercises*, etc.

4. Articulations: Slow detaché tonguing with diaphragm pulses — faster mixed, double and triple tonguings on single notes and scale passages — Altès, *26 Selected Studies*, etc.

5. Technique: Slow motion finger action graduated to trill speed — Taffanel-Gaubert scale, interval and arpeggio patterns from *Exercices Journaliers* — Moyse, *Gammes et Arpeges*, etc. Wummer, *12 Daily Exercises*, etc.

6. Etudes: (see listing on page 82.)

7. Solos— Repertoire — Orchestra Studies: (See Appendix C.)

II. Materials

Have all your materials at hand; they should include the following:

1. Soft pencil (for marking breathing points).
2. Tuning bar — or at least a tuning fork.
3. A reliable metronome.
4. A mirror for examining posture, finger position and embouchure.
5. A straight chair (alternate standing and sitting when practicing).
6. A music manuscript book (for notes and special fingerings).

The following quick reference sources should also be available:

1. *Table of Fingerings for the Boehm Flute,* E. Wagner (Carl Fisher, N.Y., 1928).
2. *A Modern Guide to Fingerings for the Flute,* J. Pellerite (Zalo Pub., Bloomington, Ind., 1972).
3. *Dictionary of Musical Terms,* Baker (Schirmer, N.Y.).
4. *Harvard Dictionary of Music,* W. Apel (Harvard Univ. Press).
5. Small Italian, German and French pocket dictionaries.

Indispensible are the catalogues of flute repertoire:

1. *Flute Repertoire Catalogue,* F. Vester (Musica Rara, London, 1967).
2. *A Handbook of Flute Literature,* J. Pellerite (Zalo Pub., Bloomington, Ind., 1965).
3. *A General Catalogue of Flute Music,* Murumatsu (Trio Assoc., Culver City, Calif., 1972).

The student should have some curiosity about the history and development of his instrument and about the styles of the different periods of musical history:

1. *On Playing the Flute,* Quantz-Reilly (Free Press, N.Y., 1966).
2. *The Flute and Flute Playing,* Boehm-Miller (Dover Pub., N.Y., 1922, reprint 1964).
3. *The Flute,* R. Rockstro (Musica Rara, London, 1890, reprint 1967).
4. *The Flute,* P. Bate (W. W. Norton & Co., N.Y., 1969).
5. *Artistic Flute, Technique & Study,* R. Stevens (Highland Music Co., Calif.).
6. *The Flutist's Guide,* F. Wilkins (Artley, Inc., Elkhart, Ind., 1957).
7. *Illustrated Method for the Flute,* Stokes-Condon (Trio Assoc., Culver City, Calif., 1971).
8. *Special Effects for the Flute,* Stokes-Condon (Trio Assoc., Culver City, Calif., 1971).
9. *New Sounds for Woodwind,* B. Bartolozzi (Oxford Univ. Press, London, 1967).
10. *Flute Forum,* A review published by W. T. Armstrong Co., Elkhart, Ind.

Of more general musical interest are:

1. *Woodwind Instruments & Their History,* A. Baines (W. W. Norton & Co., N.Y., 1957).
2. *Musical Instruments Through the Ages,* A. Baines (Broude Bro., N.Y., 1949).
3. *The History of Music in Performance,* F. Dorian (W. W. Norton & Co., N.Y., 1966).
4. *The Orchestra from Beethoven to Berlioz,* A. Carse (Broude Bro., N.Y., 1949).
5. *Bach's Ornaments,* Emory (Novello).
6. *Form and Performance,* I. Stein (Alfred A. Knopf, N.Y., 1962).

C. THE FLUTIST'S REPERTOIRE

    The following repertoire is listed to direct students toward only the most basic and standard works for the flute and to assist them in starting a well balanced library of flute literature.

    Music is expensive, not all of it good, and the publications are becoming increasingly vast. Wise students will save money and space by exploring the available music school, conservatory and public libraries for music to determine what they can perform with conviction and enthusiasm. The extensive flute recordings and frequent broadcasts of flute recitals will also help students decide what is worth purchasing and adding to their libraries.

Etudes

Altès, H.	26 Selected Studies
Andersen, J.	(Ops. 37, 41, 21, 33, 30, 15, 63, 60)
Bach, J. S.	24 Concert Studies
Berbiguier, B. T.	18 Exercises
Bitsch, M.	12 Etudes
Boehm, T.	24 Caprice Etudes, Op. 26
Bozza, E.	14 Etudes - Arabesques
Castérède, J.	12 Etudes
Cavally, Robert	Melodious & progressive Studies
Demersseman, J.	50 Etudes, Op. 4
Genzmer, H.	24 Modern Studies (2 vols.)
Hugues, L.	40 Studies, Op. 75
Jeanjean, P.	Etudes Modernes
Karg-Elert, S.	30 Capricen, Op. 107
Maquarre, A.	Daily Exercises
Moyse, M.	Gammes et Arpegès De la Sonorité
Paganini-Herman	24 Caprices
Schade, W.	24 Caprices
Taffanel-Gaubert	17 Grands Exercises journaliers
Wagner, E.	24 Concert Etudes
Wummer, J.	12 Daily Exercises

Sonatas

Albinoni, Thomasso
Bach, C. P. E.
Bach, J. C.
Bach, J. S.

Bach, W. F.
Burton, Eldin
Danzi, Franz
Devienne, Francois

Sonatas — continued

Frederick the Great of Prussia
Genzmer, Harald
Handel, George Frederick
Hindemith, Paul
Leclair, Jean Marie
Loeillet, Jean Baptiste
Marcello, Benedetto
Martinu, Bohuslav
Milhaud, Darius
Mozart, Wolfgang Amadeus
Piston, Walter
Platti, Giovanni
Poulenc, Francis

Prokofiev, Serge
Purcell, Daniel
Quantz, Johann Joachim
Reynolds, Verne
Telemann, George Philipp
Vinci, Leonardo

Sonatinas

Bitsch, Marcel
Boulez, Pierre
Dutilleux, Henri
Heiden, Bernhard

Concerti

Albinoni, Tomasso
Bach, C. P. E.
Bach, J. C.
Bach, J. S.
Boccherini, Luigi
Danzi, Franz
Gretry, Andre
Ibert, Jacques
Leclair, Jean Marie
Mozart, W. A.
Nielsen, Carl
Pergolesi, Giovanni B.
Quantz, Johann J.
Reicha, Anton
Telemann, Georg Philipp
Tomasi, Henri
Vivaldi, Antonio

Concertinas

Chaminade, Cecile
Grovlez, Gabriell
Tomasi, Henri

Suites

Bach, J. S.
Block, Ernest
Telemann, Georg Philipp
Widor, Charles Marie

Unaccompanied Solos

Amram, David	Overture and Allegro
Bach, C. P. E.	A Minor Sonata
Bach, J. S.	A Minor Sonata
Bennett, Richard Rodney	Sonatina
Bennett, Richard Rodney	A Flute at Dusk
Berio, Luciano	Sequenza
Bozza, Eugene	Image
Debussy, Claude Achille	Syrinx
Fukushima, Kasuo	Mey
Fukushima, Kasuo	Deux Kadha
Fukushima, Kasuo	Requiem
Hindemith, Paul	Acht Stücke
Honegger, Arthur	Danse de la Chevre
Ibert, Jacques	Piecè
Nielsen, Carl	The Children are Playing
Nielsen, Carl	The Fog is Lifting
Rivier, Jean	Oiseaux Tendres
Telemann, George Philipp	12 Fantasies
Verèse, Edgar	Density 21.5

Accompanied Solos

Andersen, Joachim	Scherzino
Barber, Samuel	Canzone
Bizet, George	Minuet (from L'Arlesienne)
Bozza, Eugene	Argrestide
Caplet, Andre	Reverie et Petite Valse
Casella, Alfredo	Sicilienne et Burlesque
Debussy, Claude	Le Petit Berger
	En Bateau (Petite Suite)
	Menuet
	First Arabesque

(Accompanied Solos - continued)

Enesco, Georges	*Cantabile et Presto*
Faure, Gabriel	*Fantasie*
	Pièce
Fukushima, Kasuo	*Three Pieces from Chu-u*
Gabaye, Pierre	*Etude pour Rive*
Ganne, Louis	*Andante et Scherzo*
Gaubert, Philippe	*Fantasie*
Gluck, Christoph W.	*Scene from "Orpheus"*
Godard, Benjamin	*Suite (Allegretto, Idylle, Valse)*
Gossec, Francois J.	*Gavotti*
Griffes, Charles T.	*Poem*
Grovlez, Gabriel	*Romance et Scherzo*
Hanson, Howard	*Serenade*
Hovhaness, Alan	*Dance of Black-Haired Mountain*
Hue, Georges	*Fantasie*
	Nocturne et Gigue
Ibert, Jacques	*Jeux*
	Histoires
Kennan, Kent	*Night Sililoquy*
Kuhlau, Friedrich	*Six Divertissements (Op. 68)*
Messiaen, Olivier	*Le Merle Noir*
Mozart, Wolfgang A.	*Andante in C*
Saint-Saens, Camille	*Air de Ballet d'Ascanio*
Schubert, Franz P.	*Introduction, Theme et Variations*

D. DIFFERENCE TONES

Difference Tones

Difference tones result from beats caused by the interference between two notes. When the interval is sufficient and the resultant beats become rapid enough, these difference tones have a frequency in their own right and sound as third notes, although at a much reduced volume and always lower than that of the higher note of the interval.

Consequently they are more often than not ignored by the ear but, because of the high frequencies of the flute, are quite discernible as third notes—particularly in the flute obbligato and coloratura voice combinations. They also can be quite troublesome in tuning some high sustained chords where difference tones sometimes conflict with existing scored notes, as in the final chords of Strauss's *Thus Spake Zarathustra*.

The pitch of the difference tone is determined by subtracting the lower from the upper frequency of an interval. To tune an interval properly the difference tone must be tuned also (curiously an interval of a minor 3rd will automatically supply a major root two octaves below).[1] Listen carefully to the difference tones in the following simple example and adjust the tuning of the intervals accordingly:

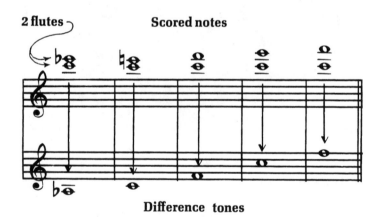

Difference tones

The following is what might be called a Trio For Two Flutes. Some of the difference tones are more discernible than others, but they are all there.

[1] For more detail consult John Redfield's chapter on Harmonic Possibilities in his book, *Music: A Science And An Art* (Tudor Pub. Co.: New York, 1937).

TRIO FOR TWO FLUTES*

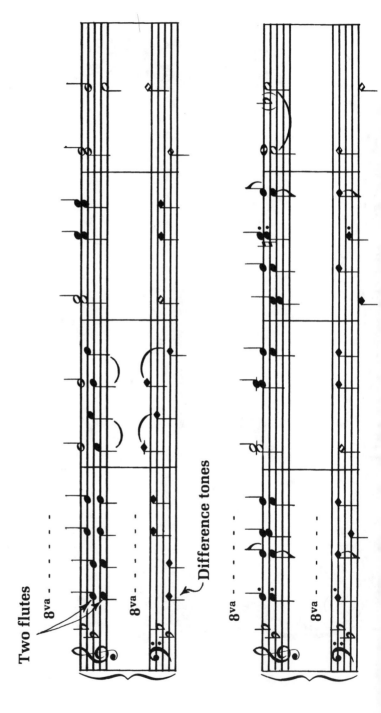

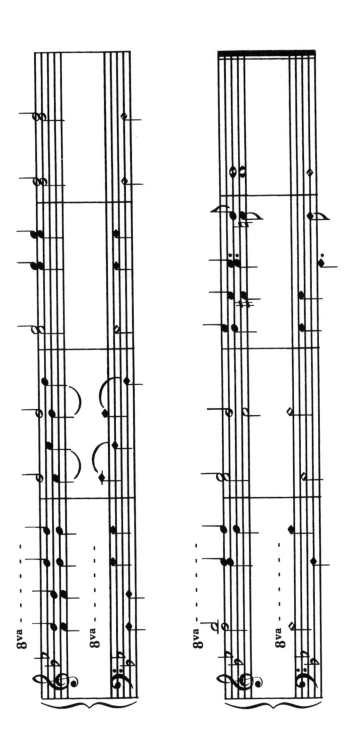

*Courtesy of Russell S. Howland

E. THE PICCOLO: AN ARTIST'S APPROACH

There are perils involved in playing the piccolo, but there are also many rewards. Moreover, with the "population explosion" in the sheer number of flutists these days, you will find yourself more in demand than a correspondingly good flutist.

The piccolo is a conspicuous voice that soars above the main body of the band or orchestra. You are a soloist whose sound, without forcing, is not lost or absorbed in the general anonymity of the ensemble. Because of the miniature finger work involved, the technique is easier and you will find the florid passages easier to play. The smaller opening in the embouchure requires less breath, so you will be able to play longer lines and compromise less with the breathing problem of the flute.

When the woodwind section is charging in "tutta forza" in a technical "tutti" passage and, to an extent, is blanketed by the total sound, the singular piccolo *is* heard and is obliged to play all the notes. There is no place to hide, and that is precisely the occupational hazard—and joy—in trying to make a musical instrument out of the shrill and puckish piccolo.

Ideally, the piccolo is a little flute and serves as an extension of the flute range—the low register of the piccolo should match the second octave of the flute and carry on up to its high C in a homogeneous scale without "shifting gears" as the octaves change. For me, and for most orchestral players, the wood piccolo, with its added resistance, more nearly matches this "flute" quality than the silver instrument, although the latter is perhaps more practical and convenient for the occasional player or the "doubler" because of its ease of playing.

Some flutists resent playing piccolo. Because of the necessary additional pressure or speed of wind, it does tend to "muscle-bind" and tense the flute embouchure. However, for those flutists who have an overly spongy, "goldfish" embouchure, an interlude on the piccolo can be a positive therapy and add a muscle tone they would not obtain otherwise. In general, I believe that those players with thinner lips are the more likely candidates for the piccolo adventure simply because it is easier for them to adjust their lips to the smaller aperture.

As to the playing, the *basic* approach is identical to that of the flute—except that the piccolo is a rather primitive instrument compared to the more domesticated and adjustable flute. In some respects it is a different instrument altogether—many have a different bore (conical),[1] a different scale, different octave relationships, and of course a different register. Because of its greatly reduced size, all of the adjustments you make are magnified and all of your movements are critical.

There is much to be said about the psychological approach to the instrument. Due to the exposure, many piccolo players try to play it "cool" and "pussy-foot" their way through the literature, but this invites trouble. The support and speed of wind will drop and so will the pitch *and* the quality. The piccolo, like the trumpet, should be heard and must be played with a kind of aggressive assurance. In some instances you must actually lead the woodwind section.

By far the greatest problem in playing the piccolo is in the tuning of the instrument in its delicate and sensitive upper registers. The player works with frequencies that accumulate in ratios so that, as he ascends, the "tonal target" becomes narrower and narrower; that is, the vibrations become so great (3,520 cycles per second for the top A) that the slightest alteration in pitch in a unison or octave will start the "beats" chattering in your ear. *For this reason it is best not to double piccolos unless absolutely necessary.* To complicate the situation further, most piano tuners "stretch" the upper octaves on that instrument; consequently, the ear comes to expect this sharpness, which makes pianissimo sustaining on the piccolo all the more difficult, for the tendency, of course, is for the pitch to drop. Similarly, the pitch tends to rise disproportionately in the fortissimos. To compensate for this, I pull out the headjoint in extended forte passages and push in for the delicately sustained pianissimos together with changes in the direction of the air stream—down for the fortissimos and more across for the pianissimos. In tuning unisons or octaves with other instruments, make your adjustments slowly and do not overcompensate. Players frequently pass each other in the process—even a slight movement of the head can alter the pitch. The "throat" tones (B, C, C$^\sharp$) tend to be sharp in the lower octave and flat in the middle—I sometimes use the harmonic fingerings for these notes in the middle octave, but the tuning of these varies from instrument to instrument, so you must find those that work for you.

Always warm up the instrument before playing (I keep mine inside my jacket pocket), *and never warm up a cold wood piccolo by blowing into it;* the different rates of expansion between the interior bore and outside diameter can disastrously check or crack the body of the piccolo.

It is recommended to gently blow air into a metal piccolo with the finger holes closed to bring the instrument up to pitch. This is not advised with a wood piccolo.

You will find it very instructive and revealing to play scales and passages in *unison* with a sympathetic flute colleague—after first being reasonably sure that *his* tuning is reliable! And if there are precarious tunings with other winds or strings in a particular composition, do as all professional musicians do—test them in private before the concert so you will know where to "place" your pitch.

The basic problem, of course, is to play the instrument in tune with *itself*, so slow scale warm-ups are essential, listening *acutely* to the pitch relationships so that the minute embouchure corrections become *automatic*. My teacher, the great William Kincaid, prescribed the following melodic minor pattern for me, and it has become part of my pre-concert warm-up ritual. Practice it the hard way—forte in the low register and pianissimo at the top:

For the sake of control, I put a very conspicuous alignment line on the head and body so that I have the same angle to work with every day and also to make it easy to push, pull, and align the tuning slide in a hurry. Again, because of the "miniaturization," the placement of the instrument on the lower lip is crucial to the pitch and the quality and should be done with great care and deliberation—the flute fits more easily and naturally into the indentation of the jaw. I perch the piccolo headjoint a bit higher on the lip than the flute (to avoid smothering the embouchure hole) and generally direct the air more *into* the instrument and *at* the opposite wall than directly across[2] to obtain a so-called "darker" quality and also to avoid the chronically shrill, sharp, and piercing tone so often painfully associated with the piccolo.

There is a difference in response of some notes on the piccolo. The top G♯ requires extra pressure of the wind and will not speak easily without the clumsy addition of two fingers of the right hand (see illustration), and the top (B♭), B, and C all require that you raise the little finger of the right hand.

All of this complicates the technique in rapid passages, and sometimes even the movement of the fingers will "jiggle" the embouchure out of adjustment. For reasons of smoothness, I sometimes swirl up on fast runs in the top register by overblowing the left hand (e.g., in A Major—A B C# D [A B C#] A). Every piccolo, by the way, must have a high B natural that speaks because there is just too much literature being written that involves it—occasionally pulling the head joint a bit will facilitate the response of this particular note.

But what really strikes terror in the heart of a piccolo player are the high, sustained pianissimos he is obliged to play. Prokofiev and Shostakovich are particularly fond of them. Over the years, I have learned that the secret (if there is one) is to relax the lips and let the air do the work. That is, keep the peripheral muscles of the embouchure firm but the cushion of the center soft, relaxed and slightly pursed forward, using a firm diaphragm in the meantime to support the flow of air. On the other hand, if you "bite" the air too hard, you will create a tension that is likely to set up self-defeating tremors in the embouchure muscles.

The vibrato situation is essentially the same as that of the flute. I like to graduate the speed of the vibrato through the range of the instrument—that is, slower in the low register and faster in the high register. Because of the higher range of the instrument, I use a faster vibrato in the top register than I ever would use on the flute. It is important to control the "width" or amplitude of the vibrato; a heavy, wide vibrato will sometimes upset the ensemble tuning, and some calm, quiet passages require just the merest hint of a vibrato.

The articulation problems differ from the flute only in that the added pressure of the air striking the lips requires more resistance to keep them from buzzing. It does take a lot of strength in the lips just to hold them apart! I use little "kicks" of the diaphragm behind the tongue for the dynamic attacks and "nudges" for the more gentle types. It is important to remember that the diaphragm and the abdominal muscles *generate* the sound and that the tongue is merely a valve to release this generated pressure.

There are no piccolo methods as such, and no one really gives piccolo lessons. For study materials, it is best to borrow and adapt those of the flute literature that avoid the extreme ranges. The Berbiguier, Hugues and Andersen etudes are good, plus the indispensable calisthenics of the Taffanel-Gaubert *Daily Exercises*. Particularly valuable to me are the vocalise-like patterns of the André Maquarre *Daily Exercises*. Memorize them, for the transpositions are a wonderful exercise for the ear.

Because the piccolo requires much smaller *amounts* of breath than the flute, it is fun to play the long lines of the baroque sonatas without gasping. Get the convenient Lea Pocket Scores of the Handel and Bach sonatas and make your own editions from the original. Many of us cut our teeth on the old-fashioned "birdcall" polkas popular in the early band-in-the-park days, but outside of these, there is practically no solo literature for the piccolo at all. There *are* three beautiful Vivaldi Concerti (two in C major and one in A minor), but all else must again be adapted from the appropriate flute literature.

Finally, it is just good, clean, extrovertish fun to plunge into a good orchestral or band "tutti" and, to an extent, ride the sound like a surfer rides out the breakers. So have fun, and lots of luck.

[1] Many piccolos are made with a cylindrical bore like the flute, but the tone quality of the conical is generally judged superior.

[2] Of course, this direction of air varies with the register and the interval.

This article was originally published as a pamphlet by W. T. Armstrong Company, Elkhart, Indiana.

F. "WILLIAM M. KINCAID"
FROM *THE FLUTIST*, JUNE 1925

Biographical

William M. Kincaid

IT IS a great pleasure for us to present to our readers this month a sketch of the life of one of America's most noted native flutists. To know William M. Kincaid is a privilege; to hear him, a treat. At the Editor's request, he prepared the following sketch, which is all too brief.

"I was born April 26, 1897, in Minneapolis, Minnesota. At the age of six months I did not show any aptitude for music beyond a pair of good lungs. When I was three years old my parents moved to Honolulu and I went with them to bring them up in the way all good parents should be brought up. My father, being a Presbyterian minister, thought my guiding hand would be needed. We lived there for about eight years, during which time I began to take lessons on the piano and the flute.

"My father's health failing him, due to tropical climate, we returned to the States and made our home in Charlotte, N. C., where my father became pastor of the First Presbyterian Church, and I continued to study the flute in a more serious manner.

"After the death of my father in 1911, I went to New York City and entered the Institute of Musical Art in order that I might have the privilege of studying under that great artist and teacher of the flute, George Barrere. My teacher in theory and counterpoint was Dr. Goetschius, and in ear training, Franklin Robinson. I graduated from the regular course at the Institute in 1914, and from the Artist's Course with highest honors in 1918, winning the medal.

"In 1914 I was engaged as assistant first flute by the New York Symphony Orchestra, playing with that organization until the spring of 1918 when I enlisted in the U. S. Navy at Pelham Naval Station. After spending nearly a year in the service I was released and in the fall of 1919 was engaged by the New York Chamber Music Society with which I played for two years, touring the entire United States and a part of Canada.

"For the past four years, I have been first flute with the Philadelphia Symphony Orchestra appearing as soloist with this orchestra and playing the *Fantasie* of Hue and the *B Minor Suite* of Bach. At present I am instructor of flute at the Curtis Institute and the Swarthmore School of Music. In addition to my pupils in these institutions, I have a large private class.

"During the summer months I go to Little Sebago Lake in Maine and spend most of my time fishing, swimming and

WILLIAM M. KINCAID

sailing. This sort of recreation enables me to go through a very strenuous season.

"During this past season I have taken part in some 200 performances which range from symphony concerts, opera performances and chamber music concerts to playing solos in recitals.

"I hope that you will find the facts which I have had the audacity to put down, useful to you, and also please permit me to become a subscriber to your most worthy magazine, THE FLUTIST. I have intended to become one for a long time, but being by nature a profound procastinator, I have neglected doing so."

—*New York, N. Y.*

G. INTERVIEW WITH WILLIAM KINCAID, MAY 1960

On February 12, when Leopold Stokowski conducted the Philadelphia Orchestra for the first time in nineteen years, he faced only one first-desk player whom he had directed during his tenure with that orchestra from 1912 to 1938. This was the solo flutist, William Kincaid. This moving reunion of great talents had an added poignancy in that the news of Kincaid's retirement had just reached the musical world.

During the years, Kincaid, from his place almost in front of the conductor's podium, has become a symbol of the Philadelphia Orchestra's special characteristics—its verve, its flexibility, its integrity. His glowing face topped with a bush of light hair, his blue eyes, his quick glance, are as familiar to Philadelphia concertgoers as William Penn atop the Court House—and as much a part of Philadelphia's tradition. In his thousands of performances as orchestra member and in his hundreds of appearances as soloist with the orchestra, Mr. Kincaid has not only furthered the orchestra's reputation but has also introduced new compositions and has widened the concept of flute playing. It is natural that the orchestra's composer-violinist Louis Gesensway, who has written a work for Kincaid, should say of his playing, "Listening to that flute-playing year in and year out has been my training in writing for the instrument. For me the flute is inseparable from Kincaid's playing of it."

Thus when news got around that Mr. Kincaid was to retire as solo flutist of the Philadelphia Orchestra at the end of the current season, deep regret was voiced not only by those closely associated with him in the musical world, but by the public at large. "What's this I hear about Mr. Kincaid's leaving the orchestra?" a policeman at Broad and Chestnut streets in Philadelphia asked an orchestra member hurrying to rehearsal at the Academy of Music.

"That news about Kincaid retiring—it's not true, is it?" a clerk at the soda counter across the way queried anxiously.

"Things just won't be the same!" was the sentiment echoed at afternoon teas and cocktail parties.

When William Kincaid made one of his recent visits to New York, where the Philadelphia Orchestra plays semi-monthly concerts during the season, I was able to put a few questions to him about his retirement.

What were the highlights of your thirty-nine years with the Philadelphia Orchestra?

"Every day was a highlight. I don't remember being bored in all the thirty-nine years. I sometimes think, when we repeat well-known works, 'Oh do I have to go over that again?' Then things start—and it's as if I'd never played it before."

What were the incidents leading up to your taking the position in the first place?

"It was in January, 1921. I was out on the coast playing with the New York Chamber Music Society, with which I toured the entire United States and a part of Canada. I got a telegram saying that Stokowski would like to see me when I came East again. I was not long in taking him up on the invitation. I met him, played for him, and by April 18 was part of the orchestra. First job was a recording for Victor. We went over to Camden for it. Recording dates were curious affairs, then—horns coming out from all over the place, the soloist sticking his head practically into one of them."

Stokowski's Interpretations

What aspects of Stokowski's conducting stand out most clearly?

"It's hard to say. Stokowski's interpretations are uniquely his. He started out his career as an organist, and an organist uses registrations as he sees fit. Stokowski wants results that have never been heard of or asked for before. He uses few words, but he gets those results. Another memorable feature in those twenty years I played under him was the number of new works he put on. Almost every program had a controversial composition. He put on *Wozzeck* at the Metropolitan Opera House with special trains taking the orchestra to and from New York. But most interesting was the way he developed the orchestral sound. I think one might say if there had been no Stokowski there would have been no orchestral sound as we know it today. It can be said Stokowski invented the Philadelphia Orchestra.

"It's to Eugene Ormandy's credit that he could take over after so individualistic a conductor. He not only has retained the good points of the orchestra but has increased its abilities and its prestige."

What about some of the other conductors under whom you have played?

"When I was with the New York Symphony (1914-1918) I played under Walter Damrosch, a man of great dignity and temperance even in his conducting. I remember his tempos were inclined to be slow. But everything moved at a slower pace in those days. I played later under Toscanini. He gave meticulous care to what the composer had written. His interpretations were clear-cut—etchings in black and white. Monteux is a warm, yet precise conductor, and he has the Gallic flair. Sir Thomas Beecham's music is easy music, without any fuss. 'Have a good start and a good ending and the middle will take care of itself,' he says. He has such a good time that it's infectious."

I understand that two compositions have been written especially for you and that you played them with the Philadelphia Orchestra.

"Yes—Concerto for Flute, by Louis Gesensway and 'Poeme' by Frederick Waltmann, The Gesensway work was originally commissioned by Dimitri Mitropoulos who was then conductor of the Minneapolis Symphony. However, he released his rights to it, when, in 1947, Ormandy wanted to conduct it with the Philadelphia Orchestra. The work is tremendously difficult. Every measure has a different metrical pattern and uses high partials which had never before been attempted by the flute in public orchestral performance. It took me a whole summer to memorize it. I did it up at our lodge in Maine. My wife didn't hear me practicing, and she'd look out of the window, and there I'd be, sitting in the hammock, just looking at the music, studying it."

Incidentally music critic Irving Kolodin wrote of Kincaid's performance of the Gesensway work, in the *New York Sun* for November 20, 1946, "It was an uncanny demonstration of the variety of tone and nuance that can be commanded on an instrument so ordinarily a monochrome as the flute. In fact, Kincaid did everything on it, virtually, but play double stops." Louis Biancolli wrote in the *New York World-Telegram*, "Actually it might have been more fitting to list the novelty as "Concerto for Kincaid and Orchestra." Whether any less-inspired flute could carry the concerto is a moot point."

Your teaching career has been as extensive as your orchestral career, has it not?

"I've been with the Curtis Institute of Music since its founding. In fact, I might be said to have been there *before* it started, since I was connected with the Settlement Music School, its predecessor, from 1923. When the Curtis Institute opened its doors in 1925 I was the only wind instrument teacher. I shall continue my teaching there after my retirement from the orchestra, and my private teaching in Philadelphia and in New York City.

A Distinguished List

Which of your pupils have especially distinguished themselves?

"It is impossible to give a complete list here. However, the following have become prominent as orchestra members or as recitalists: Julius Baker, Bach Aria Group; Harold Bennett, first flute, Metropolitan Opera Orchestra; Doriot Anthony Dwyer, first flute, Boston Symphony; Byron Hester, first flute, Houston Symphony; Britton Johnson, first flute, Baltimore Symphony; Joseph Mariano, first flute, Rochester Philharmonic; Emil Opava, first flute, Minneapolis Symphony; Donald Peck, first flute, Chicago Symphony; James Pellerite, first flute, Philadelphia Orchestra (beginning this Fall); Kenneth Scutt, first flute, New Orleans Philharmonic; Elaine Shaffer, recitalist (has concertized in the United States, Canada and Europe); Maurice Sharp, first flute, Cleveland Orchestra; Felix Skowronek, first flute, Seattle Symphony; Albert Tipton, first flute, Detroit Symphony; Robert Willoughby, first flute, Cincinnati Symphony."

The entire flute section of the Philadelphia Orchestra—Robert F. Cole, John C. Krell and Kenton F. Terry—are Mr. Kincaid's students.

Retirement with Reservations

How do you feel about retiring when you are still obviously in your prime?

"I didn't choose to retire. It's mandatory, you know—retirement at sixty-five in the Philadelphia Orchestra. I believe it's the only orchestra that has this ruling. Still, our schedule has been getting more and more strenuous; there are more and more tours and longer ones. Accommodations in some of the foreign countries leave much to be desired. Russia especially. The food situation behind the Iron Curtain is terrible. No fresh vegetables. No fresh fruit. Yet one sees from the train windows all those miles and miles of fine agricultural country. But the means of land cultivation are so primitive—farmers pushing their wooden plows. Makeshifts. Those fine tractors and that up-to-date farm machinery at the Moscow fair—I doubt the farmers know how to use them.

"The touring itself is strenuous. I always get a room to myself. Even so—things are getting harder, and at my age they ought to be getting easier.

"However, I'm not happy to leave..."

Thousands of music lovers all over the country are with you in that. They are not happy to have you leave, Mr. Kincaid.

Hope E. Stoddard

Reprinted courtesy of *The International Musician,* May, 1960.

Kincaid relaxing at his summer cottage in Raymond, Maine, 1959.

H. REMINISCENCES OF WILLIAM KINCAID
Kenton Terry

It is likely that for the half century or more of his musical life, no one exerted a greater influence on the American flute playing fraternity than William Morris Kincaid. His skill and artistry as a performer and his success as a teacher were well known and acclaimed throughout the United States and many countries abroad.

William Kincaid was born on April 26, 1895 in Minneapolis, Minnesota. His father, a Presbyterian minister, was later to accept pastorates in Hawaii, North Carolina, and Virginia. Some of young Billy's happiest childhood memories were of Hawaii, where he learned to love swimming, boating, and all water sports.

I do not recall that Mr. Kincaid ever spoke at length of early flute teachers, but obviously there were some, as his progress on that instrument was such that after his graduation from high school he was accepted as a pupil by Georges Barrère at the Institute of Musical Art (now known as the Juilliard School). Successful studies with Barrère led to Kincaid's being engaged by the New York Symphony Orchestra, where he played alongside his famous teacher. Kincaid remained with this organization until joining the New York Chamber Music Society, and it was while he was on tour with this group that a wire came from Leopold Stokowski suggesting that they meet on Kincaid's return to New York. This in turn led to his being engaged as solo flutist with the Philadelphia Orchestra, an association that would continue for the next thirty-nine years. I am sure that these years were the happiest of all for Mr. Kincaid, as his great love was orchestra playing, and with this excellent orchestra he soon developed into one of the finest first flutists of his time. His platinum flute, the shock of white hair, and his dignified yet friendly manner and appearance became a symbol of the Philadelphia Orchestra. His solo appearances with the orchestra numbered in the hundreds, and his playing of such incidental orchestra solos as the Mendelssohn Scherzo, *L'Après-midi d'un Faune*, Brahms's Fourth Symphony, and *Daphnis and Chloë* became examples of interpretation that served to inspire many young flutists. It is a pity that the quality and durability of recordings of that period were such that few examples of Kincaid's artistry remain today.

My association with Mr. Kincaid began about 1924, when I was fortunate to have him accept me as a pupil. Until that time, I was self-taught, and my only conception of flute sound was gained from listening to phonograph records. It was a revelation to listen to my teacher play at my lessons and to realize that my chosen instrument could be more beautiful than I had ever imagined. Mr. Kincaid's success as a teacher soon rivaled his reputation as a player, and his association with the Curtis Institute of Music brought him many talented students from all over the United States.

Many of these former students are now to be found in our major symphony orchestras. It is probable that during his long career his method of teaching may have changed, so I will write only of the period between 1924 and 1932. Lesson assignments consisted of Andersen etudes and solos ranging from Handel and Bach to the current Paris Conservatory solos. Much of the "daily exercise" portion of the Taffanel-Gaubert method had to be committed to memory, a feat that most of us thought to be a bore. Mr. Kincaid had a phenomenal memory. Just name opus number and key of any Andersen etude and he could play it letter perfect from beginning to end. I'm sure we all admired his ability to do this, but I'm afraid that few of us were able to match his performance.

Kincaid was always very encouraging even while being very demanding, and no one thought of going to a lesson unprepared. He had a knack for finding the right words to make a point and above all, for me, using his playing to further illustrate his point of view. Great emphasis was placed on note grouping and phrasing, and since Kincaid's thinking along these lines was comparable to that of Marcel Tabuteau, the great French oboist, Curtis students were treated to double doses of this fare. Many tales have been told of rivalry and feuds between Kincaid and Tabuteau. They make good stories, but I believe they are greatly exaggerated. These two men were musical giants in the field of orchestral playing. I'm sure they enjoyed seeing who could turn a better phrase in any given composition, but I'm equally sure that there was a mutual respect between them as well as a genuine friendship.

It was my privilege to play beside Mr. Kincaid during his last seventeen years in the Philadelphia Orchestra, and I never ceased to marvel at his enthusiasm for his work. The hundredth performance of the Beethoven Seventh Symphony or the Brahms Fourth would be played with as much attention to every detail as though it were a new piece. His ability to avoid the boring moments of a rehearsal and to enjoy a performance to the fullest seemed to give his playing a new freshness and no doubt contributed to his greatness as an artist.

Mr. Kincaid's platinum flute was made by Verne Powell for an exhibit in the Hall of Metals at the 1939 World's Fair in New York City. At that time Kincaid was playing on a Powell silver flute, and at Mr. Powell's suggestion he went to New York to try the platinum instrument. A short test convinced him that he wanted this flute, and he purchased it at the close of the Fair. Mr. Kincaid used his platinum flute exclusively from that time on, although he once admitted to me that whenever he experienced any embouchure trouble he would play a bit on his Louis Lot, and then everything would be fine again. I recall the aforementioned Lot, and it was this flute Mr. Kincaid played when I first met him. I loved the brilliance of its sound. I believe that its less-than-perfect scale caused him to switch to the Powell.

I do not think Mr. Kincaid would have enjoyed the fifty-two-week orchestral season. His summers were spent at his home on Little Sebago Lake near Raymond, Maine. He looked forward to this vacation period as a chance for relaxation and perhaps a time in which to learn new music or prepare a new solo to perform with the orchestra. Eventually, students clamoring for summer lessons led him to devote a couple of mornings a week to teaching, but it is likely that this was not a great chore in the relaxed Maine atmosphere.

I'm sure that all who knew Mr. Kincaid would agree that he was a great student of the flute, and that in spite of his love for this instrument his love of music was even greater. He took great pride in making music and not just playing the flute. His convictions were strong, but he believed that progress often led to different methods and solutions to problems. For this reason he was reluctant to do any writing or editing. Robert Cole, John Krell, and I tried on many occasions to convince him that he owed it to future generations of flutists to edit the Bach and Handel sonatas, but it was not until his retirement from the Philadelphia Orchestra that, in collaboration with Claire Polin, he did publish a flute method and edit six Bach sonatas.

Mr. Kincaid's retirement from the orchestra was not his choice, but was forced on him by a mandatory retirement policy. He planned to remain active in music by pursuing a limited career as a recitalist and, of course, continued to be in great demand as a teacher. Unfortunately, all these plans for recitals had to be cancelled when he began to suffer a series of strokes. His teaching at Curtis did go on for some time, and he found that he could teach a few private pupils as well. But from this point on, his health continued to fail. His playing days had come to an end, but his interest in music and musicians never ceased When he finally was confined to his home, he still took great delight in visits from his former students and colleagues. His bedroom windows looked out on the stage door of the Academy of Music, home of the Philadelphia Orchestra, and he kept in touch by watching the comings and goings of these old friends.

Mr. Kincaid's failing health kept him confined to his apartment and finally to his bed until his death on April 24, 1967. He was buried beside his wife Helen in her family burial plot in Gaffney, South Carolina.

Perhaps the best tribute to the memory of this great artist, and one that would please him the most, is the perpetuation of his teachings by his many pupils, and in turn, their pupils—a legacy to be treasured by the world of music.

Kenton Terry was a member of the National Symphony Orchestra before joining the Philadelphia Orchestra, where he played from 1943 to 1973. He taught at Temple University, Settlement Music School, and the New School of Music in Philadelphia and was later Visiting Professor of Flute at Indiana University and the University of Illinois.

I. REMINISCENCES OF WILLIAM KINCAID
Sol Schoenbach

It is as much a privilege to write about William Kincaid as it was for me to play with him in the Philadelphia Orchestra and in the Philadelphia woodwind quintet. He was a remarkable man, really two men, but we'll concentrate on the musician mainly. My first encounter with him was at the twenty-fifth anniversary concert of the Institute of Musical Art (later merged with the Juilliard School). At our final rehearsal in Carnegie Hall Kincaid arrived with the bassoonist Ferdinand Del Negro and some others to play. His graceful solos in *Scheherezade* left an indelible impression on me and I never dreamed that someday I would be playing with him in Philadelphia.

As one of the few wind players ever to earn an artist diploma at the Institute, a seven-year course, he was thoroughly trained by Barrère on the flute and by others in theory and harmony. When we moved to Florida one of our neighbors told us that her mother was Kincaid's teacher in piano and organ in Charlotte, North Carolina, and even at an early age he showed a great aptitude for music. He often told me of his first hearing Barrère and the New York Symphony in Spartanburg, South Carolina, and leaving that concert determined to be a flutist and to study with Barrère. His mother had great faith in his future and used the last bit of her inheritance to see that he was well prepared.

He was a thorough musician who could give you an analysis of Debussy's *Syrinx* or name the chords of the last movement of Brahms's Fourth as well as any other composition that was under scrutiny. His work with the Beebe chamber music ensemble gave him plenty of chamber music knowledge and added a great deal to our quintet. On one occasion we were rehearsing the Bozza *Scherzo,* and it never sounded like more than an etude of triplets. At the next rehearsal he told us that he had noted the suggested overall time, counted all the bars, and arrived at a metronomic speed, which we then attempted. The piece came alive and became one of our favorites—nicknamed by him "the Green Hornet." He always had a methodical approach to music, yet played with flair and carried himself in a macho manner that brought attention to his playing, but never at the expense of the music.

When I was working with him on the "wife-husband" bit in the *Leonore No. 3* overture, he would point out that I was accenting the dominant, and how it was out of line with what we were trying to say. There are so many instances that come to mind, but these give you a good example of his thorough grasp of the music. He was totally committed to the art and to his flute, which he played so well. In the hundreds of concerts we played he hardly ever failed, and the few times he did were so few and far between that they also remain in my memory. He was a consummate teacher but never offered any criticism or advice unless I brought up the subject. I could tell by the back of his head that I had done something wrong, and I was indebted to him (and to Tabuteau) for any improvements I may have made. His students were numerous and successful. One day some gushy lady at the stage entrance said, "Mr. Kincaid, all your students are so wonderful!"—to which he replied, "Why not, I accept only the best!"

As for the other William Kincaid—that can best be told in the following anecdote. Our first quintet record was due to be released, and Columbia sent a writer to interview us for the blurb on the record jacket. After a Carnegie Hall concert we all went to the bar of the Wellington Hotel across the street, where the young writer said that he would like this story to have the feel of a *New Yorker* Profile. "Let's begin," he said, "with your parental background." Mason Jones said that his father was Welsh and his mother Polish. De Lancie offered that his mother was Swiss-Italian and his father English. I said my parents were Hungarian-Austrian and Gigliotti brought in his Hungarian mother and Italian father. Kincaid was silent for a few minutes and then said, "I'm half Scotch and half soda!"

Sol Schoenbach was principal bassoonist of the Philadelphia Orchestra from 1937 to 1957 and played with Kincaid in the Philadelphia Woodwind Quintet. From 1957 to 1981 he served as executive director of the Settlement Music School in Philadelphia. He has also taught at the Curtis Institute.

J. DISCOGRAPHY OF SOLO AND CHAMBER MUSIC RECORDINGS BY WILLIAM KINCAID
John Solum

Solo Recordings

J. S. Bach: Brandenburg Concerto No. 2
Philadelphia Orchestra/Leopold Stokowski, conductor; Marcel Tabuteau, oboe; other soloists unknown.
78 rpm: RCA Victor Red Seal Album M59 (1928), His Master's Voice D 1702-3. LP: dell'Arte DA 9001.

J. S. Bach: Brandenburg Concerto No. 2
Philadelphia Orchestra/Eugene Ormandy, conductor; Marcel Tabuteau, oboe; Saul Caston, trumpet; Alexander Hilsberg, violin.
78 rpm. World's Greatest Music SR 14-15 (1938)

Georg Philipp Telemann: Suite in A Minor
Philadelphia Orchestra/
Eugene Ormandy, conductor
78 rpm. RCA Victor Red Seal DM 890 (ca. 1941)

Howard Hanson: Serenade for Solo Flute, Harp, and Strings
Philadelphia Orchestra/
Eugene Ormandy, conductor
78 rpm. Columbia 12983D in album MM851

Solo Recordings — continued

**Christoph Willibald von Gluck:
Minuet and Dance of the Blessed Spirits**
from Orfeo ed Euridice
Philadelphia Orchestra /
Eugene Ormandy, conductor
78rpm. Columbia MM 894 (1949)

Kent Kennan: Night Soliloquy
Philadelphia Orchestra /
Eugene Ormandy, conductor
78 rpm. Columbia MM 940 (ca. 1949-50)

Music for the Flute by William Kincaid
Vladimir Sokoloff, piano
Marcello: Sonata in F (ed. J. Slater); Hindemith: Sonata for flute and piano; Saint-Saëns: Airs de ballet from Ascanio; Caplet: Reverie, Petite Valse; Debussy: Syrinx [LP version only]; Dutilleux: Sonatine.
78 rpm: Columbia Album MM 961. LP: Columbia ML 4339 (1950)

J. S. Bach: Brandenburg Concerto No. 5
Philadelphia Orchestra / Leopold Stokowski, conductor; Fernando Valenti, harpsichord; Anshel Brusilow, violin.
LP: Columbia ML 5713 (mono), Columbia MS 63113 (stereo) (1957). LP reissues: Odyssey Y33228 (1974); CBS Harmony 30061. CD reissue: Sony MH2K 62345 (1995)

Solo Recordings — continued

Charles T. Griffes: Poem for Flute and Orchestra on album *The Philadelphia Orchestra/First Chair*
Philadelphia Orchestra /
Eugene Ormandy, conductor
LP. Columbia ML 4629 (1965)

William Kincaid Plays the Flute—Volume 1 (Intermediate)
Vladimir Sokoloff, piano
Giovanni Benedetto Platti: Adagio and Allegro; Handel: Sonata No. 3 in G major; Charles Marie Widor: Scherzo from Suite; Christoph Willibald Gluck: Scene from Orpheus; Robert Guyn McBride: In the Groove; Handel: Sonata No. 5 in F major; Bach: Siciliano from Sonata in E-flat major for flute and harpsichord; Joachim Andersen: Scherzino; Camille Saint-Saëns: Ascanio, Airs de ballet; André Caplet: Reverie and Petite Valse
LP. Grand Award Records AAS-705 (ca. 1960)

William Kincaid Plays the Flute—Volume 2 (Advanced)
Vladimir Sokoloff, piano
W. A. Mozart: Concerto in G Major, K. 313; Bach: Sonata No. 2 [in E major, BWV 1031]; Gabriel Fauré: Fantaisie, op. 79; Kent Wheeler Kennan: Night Soliloquy; Cécile Chaminade: Concertino
LP. Grand Award Records AAS 706 (ca. 1960)

Solo Recordings — continued

W. A. Mozart: Concerto No. 1 in G for flute and orchestra, K. 313
on album *Mozart/The Four Concertos for Woodwinds and Orchestra, Vol. 1*
Philadelphia Orchestra /
Eugene Ormandy, conductor
LP: Columbia ML 5851 (mono), Columbia MS 6451 (stereo) (1963; recorded April 1960). CD reissue: Sony SM3K 47215 (1991)

William Kincaid
The National Flute Association Historic Recordings Series
Telemann: Suite in A Minor for flute and strings; Gluck: Scene from Orphée et Eurydice; Kennan: Night Soliloquy (live broadcast, 9 December 1944); Hanson: Serenade for solo flute, harp and strings; Louis Gesensway: Concerto for flute and orchestra (live broadcast, 2 November 1946).
CD: NFA-1 (1995)

Chamber Music Recordings

Janacek: Mladi (Youth Suite)
Philadelphia Woodwind Quintet (William M. Kincaid, flute; John de Lancie, oboe; Anthony Gigliotti, clarinet; Sol Schoenbach, bassoon; Mason Jones, horn), Leon Lester, bass clarinet.
LP: Columbia ML 4991 (1955)

Chamber Music Recordings — continued

Philadelphia Woodwind Quintet
(William M. Kincaid, flute; John de Lancie, oboe; Anthony Gigliotti, clarinet; Sol Schoenbach, bassoon; Mason Jones, horn).
Hindemith: Kleine Kammermusik, Op. 24, No. 2; Ibert: Trois Pièces Brèves; Bozza: Scherzo, Op. 48; Haydn: Divertimento No. 1 in B-flat major; Beethoven: Sextet in E-flat (arr. for quintet by PWWQ)
LP: Columbia ML 5093 (1956)

Schoenberg: Quintet for Wind Instruments, Op. 27
Philadelphia Woodwind Quintet
(William M. Kincaid, flute; John de Lancie, oboe; Anthony Gigliotti, clarinet; Sol Schoenbach, bassoon; Mason Jones, horn)
LP: Columbia ML 5217 (1957)

The Philadelphia Woodwind Quintet
Reicha: Quintet in E-Flat, Op. 88, No. 2
Philadelphia Woodwind Quintet
(William M. Kincaid, flute; John de Lancie, oboe; Anthony Gigliotti, clarinet; Sol Schoenbach, bassoon; Mason Jones, horn)
LP: Columbia ML 5715 (mono), Columbia MS 6315 (stereo) (1962)

Chamber Music Recordings — continued

Paul de Wailly: Aubade for flute, oboe, and clarinet
On album *Pastorales*
Philadelphia Woodwind Quintet, including William Kincaid, flute; John de Lancie, oboe; Anthony Gigliotti, clarinet
LP: Columbia ML 5984 (mono) (1964); Columbia MS6584 (stereo) (1964)

INDEX

Alternate fingerings, 11, 12, 58.
    See also Harmonic fingering
Altès, Henri: 26 Selected Studies, 76
Andersen, Joachim, 112: 24 Exercises for flute, Op. 33, 36–37, 44
Appoggiaturas, 59
Articulation, 17–22, 43, 60, 99
Bach, Johann Sebastian, 34n;
    Sonata no. 4 in C major, 35
Barrère, Georges, 110, 116
Beecham, Sir Thomas, 12n
Beethoven, Ludwig van, 46, 54
Berbiguier, Benoit Tranquille, 37
Bowing and articulation, 34, 35;
    on violin, 17–18
Brahms, Johannes, 46
Breath, 42
Breathing, 2–4, 47, 55–57
Breathing points, 55, 56
Cheeks, 5
Chopin, Frederic, 36
Conducting, 32
Cross fingering, 24
Cross rhythms, 52
Dance elements, 30
Debussy, Claude, 46
Diaphragm, 2–4, 40, 72;
    and articulation, 18, 19;
    and vibrato, 15

Difference tones, 87
Double tonguing, 20
Dynamics, 9–10, 39, 45, 57–58
Editions, 64
Embouchure, 5–7, 11, 39, 40, 41, 42, 72
Ensemble, 61
Facility, 25
Fake fingering, 58. See also Alternate fingerings, Harmonic fingering
Finger position, 23
Finger technique, 22–26, 36
Flageolett sounds, 7
Flautando, 9
French horn, 38
Gesensway, Louis, 7, 106
Grace notes, 59
Grouping, phrase, 31–38
Harmonic fingering, 11, 58
Haydn, Franz Joseph, 46
Heifetz, Jascha, 39
Intensity, 9–10, 13–14, 35, 40, 41, 42, 58; and vibrato, 16
Intonation, 12, 94–97
Kincaid, William, biography, 101–18;
    discography 119–24
Legato intervals, 38
Line, 42–47
Low register 5, 7

Mahler, Gustav, 46
Maquarre, André: *Daily Exercises*, 76, 99
Memorization, 61
Metronome, 26, 36, 52, 54
Moyse, Marcel: *De La Sonorité*, 76; *Gammes et Arpèges*, 76
Mozart, Wolfgang Amadeus, 46, 60, 65
Nature, 31
Notation, 32
Note grouping, 32, 33
Ornaments, 59
Overtone series, 38
Overtones, 8
Phrase groupings, 31–38
Phrasing, 29–47
Piccolo, 92–100
Pick-up, 55
Pivotal notes, 51
Platinum flute, 113
Practice room, 11
Rallentando, 54
Ravel, Maurice, 46
Release, 56
Repertoire, 64
Resonance, 41, 73
Rhythm, 50–53
Rhythmical subdivision, 19

Rhythmic groupings, 36
Ritard, 54, 55
Rockstro, 6n
Rubato, 36, 55, 56
Staccato, 3, 21
Strauss, Richard, 46
Stravinsky: *Sacre du Printemps*, 14
Subdivision, 50
Tabuteau, Marcel, viii, ix, xi, 21, 30, 35, 36, 41, 58, 112; numbering system, 35, 36
Taffanel–Gaubert: *Daily Exercises*, 25, 76, 99
Tempos, 53–55
Timbre, 13
Tone, 2, 3, 7, 9, 12, 13
Tonguing, 4, 18, 19
Triple tonguing, 20
Trills, 60
Tschaikowsky, Peter Illych, 46
Vibrato, 9, 14–17, 98
Violin, 2, 9, 11, 20n
Volume, 9–10
Vowel resonance, 4
Wagner, Richard, 54
Whistle tones, 7, 76
Wind velocity, 39, 40, 41
Wummer, John: *12 Daily Exercises*, 76

About the Author

John Krell was solo piccoloist and a member of the flute section of the Philadelphia Orchestra from 1952 to 1981. After graduating from the University of Michigan, he studied with William Kincaid at the Curtis Institute and later joined him as a colleague in the Philadelphia Orchestra. Mr. Krell has been an instructor of flute at the Curtis Institute of Music, the Philadelphia Musical Academy, Temple University, and the Settlement Music School. His published works include *20th Century Orchestra Studies for Flute* (G. Schirmer). Mr. Krell received the Citation of Merit from the University of Michigan, the C. Hartman Kuhn Award, given by the Philadelphia Orchestra for outstanding service, and, in 1995, the Lifetime Achievement Award of the National Flute Association. His long association with William Kincaid as a student, teaching associate, fellow performer, and friend place him in an excellent position to communicate the highlights of Kincaid's legacy to flutists throughout the world.

OTHER PUBLICATIONS SPONSORED BY THE NATIONAL FLUTE ASSOCIATION

My Complete Story of the Flute
Leonardo de Lorenzo
New introductions by
Susan Berdahl and Nancy Toff
Texas Tech University Press, 1992

***The NFA 20th Anniversary Anthology
of American Flute Music***
John Solum, editor
Oxford University Press, 1993

William Kincaid
The National Flute Association
Historic Recordings Series, 1995